THE PRACTICE
OF IMMORTALITY

THE PRACTICE OF IMMORTALITY

A Monk's Guide to Discovering Your Unlimited
Potential for Health, Happiness, and Positivity

ISHAN SHIVANAND

NEW YORK   BOSTON

Copyright © 2025 by Ishan Shivanand

Written with Sally Collings

Cover design by YY Liak. Cover illustrations: tree by Artology Namaha/Shutterstock; figure by Aninata/Shutterstock. Cover copyright © 2025 by Hachette Book Group, Inc.

Hachette Book Group supports the right to free expression and the value of copyright. The purpose of copyright is to encourage writers and artists to produce the creative works that enrich our culture.

The scanning, uploading, and distribution of this book without permission is a theft of the author's intellectual property. If you would like permission to use material from the book (other than for review purposes), please contact permissions@hbgusa.com. Thank you for your support of the author's rights.

Balance
Hachette Book Group
1290 Avenue of the Americas
New York, NY 10104
GCP-Balance.com
@GCPBalance

First Edition: May 2025

Balance is an imprint of Grand Central Publishing. The Balance name and logo are registered trademarks of Hachette Book Group, Inc.

The publisher is not responsible for websites (or their content) that are not owned by the publisher.

Balance books may be purchased in bulk for business, educational, or promotional use. For information, please contact your local bookseller or the Hachette Book Group Special Markets Department at special.markets@hbgusa.com.

Print book interior design by Sheryl Kober.

Library of Congress Control Number: 2025931457

ISBNs: 978-0-306-83456-1 (paper over board); 978-0-306-83457-8 (ebook)

Printed in the United States of America

LSC-C

Printing 2, 2025

*This book is dedicated to the divine spark that lives
in all human beings; to the gurus before me who have
helped awaken this divinity in people; and to all seekers who
are on a quest to find this divinity within themselves.*

न जायते म्रियते वा कदाचि
नायं भूत्वा भविता वा न भूयः |
अजो नित्यः शाश्वतोऽयं पुराणो
न हन्यते हन्यमाने शरीरे || 20||

The Spirit is neither born nor does it die at any time. It does not come into being or cease to exist. It is unborn, eternal, permanent, and primeval. The Spirit is not destroyed when the body is destroyed.

—The Bhagavad Gita, Chapter 2 Verse 20.

CONTENTS

Introduction   ix

Part One: Leaving Paradise

Chapter 1: Pursuing the Path of Oneness   3

Chapter 2: Chasing the Nectar of Immortality   11

Chapter 3: Becoming a Master of Time   23

Chapter 4: Connecting to the Immortal Self   37

Chapter 5: From Destruction, a Seed Grows   47

Part Two: Mastering the Mind

Chapter 6: Two Wolves, Fighting   63

Chapter 7: Forgetting Our Divine Nature   75

Chapter 8: Light My Fire with Your Candle   85

Chapter 9: Becoming Superhuman   95

Chapter 10: The Balloon Tied to Your Toe   107

Chapter 11: Drinking the Poison of Ego   115

Part Three: Mastering the Body

Chapter 12: Seeing Prana in Action   127

Chapter 13: Taking the First Steps to Immortality   143

Chapter 14: Breaking Free of Our Minds   153

Chapter 15: Finding an Anchor in Chaos   161

Contents

Chapter 16: Two Birds in a Tree　175
Chapter 17: Falling in Love with Shiva　185
Chapter 18: Chasing the Idea of Spirituality　195

Part Four: Mastering the Soul
Chapter 19: Facing the Dark Passenger　207
Chapter 20: Going Back to the Beginning　219
Chapter 21: Yoga Is Freedom in Action　229
Chapter 22: Joining the Dance of Immortality　239

Your Immortal Self　249
Glossary　251
Acknowledgments　263
About Shiv Yog and Yoga of Immortals　265

INTRODUCTION

Two birds perch on the same tree, inseparable companions. One bird eats the fruit, while the other looks on. The first bird is our finite self, feeding on the pleasures and pains of its deeds, consuming all of the anxiety, the stress, the overwhelm of this life. The second bird is our immortal, infinite self, silently and serenely witnessing all.

This book is about my journey and how I evolved from that first bird, bound by chaos, to the second bird, my immortal self. It is also about you: how you can discover that second, immortal version of yourself.

Here is a simple truth: we are not the finite beings that our limiting mindset would have us believe. Each one of us has untapped potential to not only enjoy, but to also *create* good health, success, happiness, and positivity—and to infinitely stretch, manipulate, and fully utilize the time we have been given to do it.

For most of us, the limits of our minds are most often disguised as convenience and productivity. In this modern world, we are just a Google search away from knowing what to think, say, or do. We are dependent on food, on alcohol, on drugs, on sex, on social media for

Introduction

stimulation. So, we remain in an endless sleep, unless someone calls to us—wake up!

I was raised as a Shaivite, one devoted to Shiva. One of the great Hindu deities, Shiva is known by other names: Shambho (benign), Mahesha (great lord), and Mahadeva (great god) are just a few of them. We Shaivites are oriented toward merging with Shiva, becoming one with him. In this tradition, the divine is not separate from us; it is a part of us. The universe is within us. All people already possess immortality within themselves—most are just unaware of it. I am setting out to wake them from their slumber.

I was born into an ancient lineage of yogis, and I spent the first twenty years of my life in a monastery, where each day we learned ancient yogic techniques to cultivate a strong, healthy mind and spirit. In this ashram, there were no clocks. There were no seconds, hours, days, or months; there were only seasons. When the cold winds came, we would say, "Ah! It's winter!" When we saw the birds building their nests, we would say, "Spring is here!" Our clock was our senses.

All who lived in the monastery knew of a state called *mahasiddha*, a state of unity where there is great stillness and a beautiful silence. Those rare few who were able to achieve it, themselves called *mahasiddhas*, had mastered the process and mastered themselves; they were perfect, their mortal selves completely merged with their immortal selves. They could cease dwelling on the past or worrying about the future. Time had no dominion over the mahasiddhas. That is not because they had gained any kind of magical control over the literal ticking of the seconds—they just knew a secret. The thing that makes us feel the anxiety of time moving too quickly, or the pressure of an imminent deadline, is never the actual passing of time. It is our own minds.

The monks at the monastery were not afraid of death, or disease, or anything else. They had found an affinity with the rest of the world: they were made up of the same energy as the trees, the mountains, and the lakes. They had the same hours in the day, but all the time in the world.

Yet it was when I came out of the ashram that my real spiritual journey began. Then, I came to appreciate the reality of a certain parable I had been taught in the ashram. My guru told me that glass can be either a mirror or a window. When you look in a mirror, you see only a reflection of yourself; when you look at a window, you see through it to the beauty and the infinity of the universe around you. A mirror is painted black on one side; a window is pure, unobscured. To change a mirror into clear glass, you must purify it, removing the paint. Outside the ashram, I went through a process of purification, so that finally when I looked inside I could see the second bird—my immortal self.

As I moved out into the wider world, it seemed to me that people needed a life raft. I saw students going into the world unprepared for its harshness and chaos. I saw medical professionals suffering burnout because of the weight of emotional need on their shoulders. I saw veterans torn apart by the burden of their military experiences. So many people were suffering the effects of self-harm, self-destruction, anxiety, depression, insomnia, helplessness—I wanted them all to have access to the tools that had made me stronger.

Today, I travel the world, fulfilling my teaching mission as the creator of Yoga of Immortals. The program employs an array of

Introduction

vigorous and soothing breathwork (pranayama), consciousness, mindfulness, and energy channelization techniques, built upon the wisdom of the twenty-one generations that precede me in my spiritual lineage. In the monastery, these processes were quite vague, not organized or explicitly spelled out. My life mission has been to make them more systematic so that anyone, anywhere, can learn them and put them into practice.

Although these teachings are ancient, they are by no means obsolete; they are entirely relevant to our world today. We know that the world around us is one with us, and when we destroy the world, we end up destroying ourselves. And no matter how much we rely on technology and believe that we have solved every human dilemma, sooner or later we may reach a point where we become disillusioned. That is the point where we are ready to take an inward journey—like the one I describe here, in which I evolved from the first bird to the second bird and found my immortal self.

Although my program uses the word *yoga* in its name, this is not the yoga we know from Western health clubs and fitness studios—which, to quote the wise words of another guru, "took a practice that is about the spirit and the heart, and made it about the butt." The yogic and meditative practices of my tradition encompass every limb of yoga—not just the physical aspect but also the emotional, cognitive, and interpersonal aspects. The yoga I teach is a therapeutic yoga, a practice of living life—not merely a way to improve your posture and physical flexibility. A lot of Western traditions focus on the first bird, trying to still it, rather than on merging with the second bird on the higher branch. It is in such a merging that beautiful things can happen.

When I speak of immortality, I am not speaking of some

Introduction

mythical state; I am speaking of an attitude. I am speaking of a practice. I am speaking of a wake-up call. It is not about gaining more time, but about expanding your relationship with the time you have. And that is what I offer to you as you read this book.

These ideas might sound mystical and abstract, but the core premise is not so unfamiliar—in fact, the idea of existing in the present moment is at the root of almost all popular, contemporary mindfulness practice. If we can truly live in the present moment, then we allow our anxieties about the past and the future to fall away; we relax and begin to see a little more clearly that which is directly in front of us. We become that much closer to being a mahasiddha.

I can't promise that reading this book will make you a mahasiddha—many monks spend years and even decades of daily practice working toward that goal, and still only a small percentage achieve it—but I can promise that this book, and the practices within it, will fundamentally change your relationship with time.

Though I am the son of a well-known guru and spiritual leader, I was not born any more knowledgeable or spiritually evolved than anyone else. My personal journey began with many traditional lessons, training my body and mind through yoga, meditation, martial arts, storytelling, and herbal medicine. But some of the most significant lessons I learned came through profoundly nontraditional means. My circumstances and my ego forced me to undergo my own internal pilgrimage to discover the nectar of immortality enfolded within my soul—just as every single one of us must do in our own time and as every single one of us is capable of doing with the proper guidance.

The Practice of Immortality imparts its teachings through the story of my passage from the ashram to the world outside, the transformative journey that inspired me to share the wisdom of my lineage with a world suffering the effects of anxiety, fear, competitiveness, and anger. It is also a guide to achieving immortality—just not in the way that most people think of immortality. In the Eastern meditative sciences, the crown of the head is the seat of Shiva, and the base of the spine is the seat of Shakti. In between those two points, between Shiva and Shakti, lies the whole universe. I am created from the universe, and I have the universe within me.

Consider this book an origin story. It depicts not only the origin of Ishan Shivanand, monk and teacher, now imparting my program to millions of participants, but also the origin of the program I developed by tapping into the ancient wisdom of the Vedic sciences. Even though this program is based on modalities that are thousands of years old, it can be substantiated by modern science. As the head monk of the Shiv Yog lineage, since 2008 I have taught millions of people in every country under the blue sky. Teachers are always learning from their students, so this constant interaction with people of all races, genders, and belief systems has allowed me to learn and grow, year by year. As a researcher, I have conducted quantitative studies that have demonstrated the benefits of the Shiv Yog practices in reducing anxiety, insomnia, and depression by significant measures.

Throughout the book, you will be given the tools to begin your own practice and start on your own journey. You will benefit from the lessons that my ancestors took millennia to master, but you will grasp them in *this* lifetime, enabling you to push through any turmoil—stress, fear, anger, sorrow—life sends your way.

In my culture, stories are very powerful—they are the vehicle for all teachings. The Bhagavad Gita, one of the sacred texts of Hinduism, is told as a conversation between Krishna, the lord of the universe, and the warrior-hero Arjuna. Similarly, the lessons to be found in this book are hiding in plain sight, woven through the tales of my childhood. Each chapter begins with a *sutra*, a word that literally means "thread." When we make a flower garland, we use a sutra to give it structure and form; if the thread breaks, the flowers scatter. The sutras in this book are the threads of universal truths that can be found running through each chapter.

At the end of each chapter is a meditation practice called *samadhi*. This Sanskrit word is used in many spiritual traditions to describe a state in which, through meditative concentration, the individual becomes one with the universe. Samadhi is both something you do and something you experience. It brings with it a sense of bliss, by which I mean an innate inner joy that is unaffected by our circumstances. Within this bliss there is no sorrow, fear, guilt, disappointment, worry, anger, despair, or confusion. It is available to every one of us, no matter whether we are male or female and regardless of our age, the belief system in which we were raised, or the color of our skin.

Think of these samadhi practices as the living form of the chapter that you can participate in. If the chapter is the tree, then the sutra is its seed and the practice is its fruit, offering you deep bliss as you focus upon it, meditate upon it, and learn from it.

Through these three elements—the musings of the sutras, the contemplation of the stories, the application of the meditations—there is a certain ebb and flow, just as in music there is activity and inactivity, the note played and the pause in between. If you combine the notes and the pauses, music will result. But if there is just the note, continuous without pause, then it is not music—it is noise. Today, life is often noise rather than music because we have forgotten how to pause. In this book, the story is the note, and the meditation is the pause. The entry point to your immortal self lies in that pause. So I recommend that you read one chapter, feel the resonance of the story, then pause with the meditation—and continue. In this way, you and I together can make a symphony.

There are many paths by which you can go inside and experience the harmony that lies within, setting aside the emotional burdens that you carry. My hope is that this book will offer you one such path, so that you can become connected to your immortal self and harness the power that already lies within you.

THE PRACTICE OF IMMORTALITY

PART ONE

LEAVING PARADISE
RAJASTHAN

CHAPTER 1
PURSUING THE PATH OF ONENESS

आपको ध्यायो आपको भजो
आप में आपकेराम आप होकर रहते हैं।

Meditate on the self,
Contemplate the self.
The divine that you seek lives in you as you.

In the dark mountains of Aravalli in Northwest India, the oldest mountain range in the world, huge granite rocks lie scattered about the vast landscape. There is nothing special about any one of them. One day, a man comes along, looks at a particular rock, and smiles. This man is an artist, and he feels compassion for the rock. He wants to make it special, so he picks up his tools and starts to carve it. Under the scorching sun, the relentless pounding of his hammer rings out, and it seems that the rock will be destroyed beneath his blows. But to the artist's trained eye, the rock is changing—becoming something else. As the rock transforms, meaning emerges. Now, this one rock is different from all the boulders. It is beautiful. It is a story. The creator stands back and observes his creation, a majestic shape with defined traits, each line and curve having deep significance. And the creator smiles and walks away.

Now, the rock is special. It is art. It will stand tall and give inspiration to all travelers. It will lend beauty to the landscape. It has purpose.

I was told that every child is born a rock. If the child is lucky, they meet an ascended master who sees beauty within the child. The master spends time carving the child, shaping them, giving them purpose. In the master's wisdom, the child is molded. The greater the master, the more finesse they have in their art: for this is not the first rock that the master has carved. There have been many before this one, and there will be many after, for the master is ancient: as ancient, probably, as the mountains of Aravalli.

But if the child is unlucky, they encounter no master on their travels through the world. Random hammers and chisels of traumas and negative emotions hit them from every direction, striking every surface. There is no structure; there is no design; there is no focus. And yes, by some fluke, the random beating may create a masterpiece out of the chaos. But that is a one in a billion chance—it does not happen for every child. Mostly, in the end, there is no art. What remains is just dust.

As a child of the monastery, I was the lucky one: a piece of rock born surrounded by ancient masters: great monks, each having great skill, capable of creating a masterpiece. And as far back as I can recall, through their grand design the hammer and chisel have worked their magic in my mind, body, and soul.

I remember a beautiful night sky filled with thousands of stars. In the desert where I lived, every night we slept under the open sky, and I could see the great constellations. Watching dozens of shooting stars streaking across the sky, I came to understand the magnitude of the universe. As daybreak came, across the desert I could see the silhouettes of the Aravalli mountains. On the foothills I could see men and children, leading away their caravans of camels, and with the clanging of the bells came the sounds of mystic chants all around me. The artisans and the monks, speaking a language as old as time, reciting the hymns of the Vedas: legendary scriptures, which were not crafted by any human hand. It is said these were the celestial sounds of the universe, the eternal knowledge that could be heard only once real silence was achieved. It is said that for thousands of years the Vedas were transferred as energies from the master to the disciple, once he was chiseled into perfection and enlightenment. But with the advent of word and paper, they were written down, and they could be read and memorized and taught.

I just liked the sounds. They made me vibrate. It was as if I had never awakened from my sleep, or as if I was in a deep state of hypnosis. I felt like a bee filled with the buzzing of these sacred mantras.

Then I would stand up, plant my feet in the sand, and look down at my little footprints. Such is the beauty of living in the desert: you can see footprints. Before the wind sweeps them away, just for a little time, you know who has gone where and from where they have come. I would buzz and walk and look for the biggest, deepest footprint of all: the footprint of my guru, my teacher. He was a strong man, with heavy bones and a thick black beard, and his eyes glittered with pure sunlight. This guru was the one who had taken me under his wing in the monastery. As it happened, he was also the head monk—and my father.

I called him Babaji, which means "father." It is an affectionate term but also full of respect. Babaji had a small hut, and behind it was a huge rock on which he would sit and meditate. I always knew where he would be, but still I liked to follow his footprints. I knew where he would be because he had two huge dogs. Powerful creatures, always alert, they followed my father like his shadow. One dog was called Tufan, a Sanskrit word meaning "storm," and the other was Shanti, meaning "peace." From a distance, they would see me scampering across the sand as fast as I could, and as I approached, they would stand up as if honoring me. I would walk behind the hut and see my teacher meditating.

A day came when Babaji told me, "Sit, Ishan. Let me give you your first lesson." He was about to strike me with the first blow of his hammer. I did not know it then, but I would be changed forever. For that is the ignorance of the rock, and that is the value of the hammer's strike.

He told me to close my eyes and to feel everything that was around me: the sun, the sky, the earth, the sand, the wind.

"What do you feel?" he asked me.

"I feel hungry."

I heard him laugh, but I dared not open my eyes. Discipline was the first thing taught to every child in the monastery, and the word of your guru was law. If he told me to close my eyes, then that was the order I would follow.

"Son," he said to me, "people say that God is the creator, and you are the created. But that is the path of duality. The path of separation. My dear son, God is the dancer, and you are the dance, and that is the path of oneness. I want you to sit and feel that you are one with the universe. Feel your every atom. And within each atom, the movement is the dance of God. While he dances, you exist. And when he stops, you stop. And if you can be one with this concept of nonduality—*advaita*—your consciousness will start to ascend."

Next, he told me to focus on my breath. "As you start to inhale, feel your body. Now exhale and bring that awareness up to your conscious mind. Then as you inhale again, go deeper and feel your organs. Shift that awareness from your subconscious to your conscious as you exhale. Inhale again and go even deeper; try to feel the smallest part of what you are, the atoms. Dive deep, then bring that awareness up to the surface. Then inhale a little more and try to visualize the atoms, dancing like the particles of sand dance with the wind."

Young child that I was, I started to imagine a sandstorm inside me, spinning round and round, the dance of atoms.

"This is the dance of Shiva," Babaji told me, referring to one of the most supreme deities. "Meditate on this for a moment and accept you are one with the Dancer. Feel your body. And then inhale and exhale and bring the awareness up from the atoms to the surface."

My father's voice was very powerful: a deep bass, with a strong reverberation to it. It was like music, even though he was just talking. I'm sure birds are just talking to one another, but it feels like music to one's ears. And so was the voice of my father, giving me instruction as I sat. I could hear his music.

I did not know it then, but Babaji was introducing me to one of the fundamental techniques of samadhi, allowing me to connect with the very universe.

This is how my days went as a child of the monastery. My other earliest memories are of many people sitting together and eating, all of them monks of various shapes and sizes. I do not know where they came from. Some stayed in the monastery; others were travelers who would come and go. With the monks who were passing through, we were always encouraged to sit and listen, for one of the greatest sutras—rules—of the monastery was *satsang*, which literally means "good company." The monks believed that an object at rest tends to remain at rest. It is when an outside force is applied, knowledge is given, and the sparks of cognition flare up that a person starts to transcend their own being. In satsang, the monks believed great knowledge and inspiration is achieved. What we know, we pursue, and what we do not, we remain in blissful ignorance of. There is a saying in India: a monkey doesn't know how ginger tastes, so the monkey never pursues ginger. Mount Everest has stood tall for millions of years, yet nobody cared, nobody climbed it. Then Tenzing Norgay and Edmund Hillary climbed to the summit, and suddenly, everybody wanted to climb it. Through connection with others, we discover more, become more.

In satsang, we would read, and we would listen to the monks tell us stories of their great journeys and their great pursuits. All around me, the faces of the other young students would light up with wonder and purpose. I would see the other children listening to the tales of the great monks and how they went into the deepest of the jungles to meditate under the oldest of trees, receiving the most divine light, and I would be intrigued but not inspired. I would hear about great monks who left behind riches and kingdoms and walked toward immortality, their bodies ageless, their wisdom infinite, their years uncountable, and I would be intrigued but not inspired. I would sit there in my *dhoti*—a cloth that you wore wrapped around your waist—my fingers sifting through the sand, and my father's dog Tufan resting his head in my lap. And I would wonder, *What plan did fate have for me? What would be my goal?*

At those moments I would try my father's meditation again, going deep down inside. I observed the answer lying within me, and I exhaled, bringing the awareness to my present being. It felt easy, but the trouble with "easy" is I didn't truly appreciate the value of such awareness, and I certainly didn't feel the kind of drive that I saw in all these great monks as they followed their spiritual path. The meditation benefited me, but I felt disconnected—as if I was catching the tiniest glimpse of something even more vast and beautiful.

For me, the greatest sense of satsang came with animals rather than people. When you are living with a group of monks, you are a rabbit on the ground, and you are observing birds in the sky. You can see and appreciate them, but you can only imagine what their flight must be like because they are so far removed from your reality. My true friends were the animals. In that desert landscape, things like fences didn't exist, so dogs and cows would wander around, and sometimes they would get hurt. I loved rescuing animals, so if I found an injured creature, I would look after it. One time I found a pup that had got hurt, and I was taking care of it. He was a very nice pup, but he made strange noises and had very big, odd-looking feet. One day someone came to the monastery and saw me with my pup. "Hey!" he exclaimed. "Why does that kid have a hyena?" To me, it was just like any other living being. I could understand its hunger, its lack of connection, its fear—and I could cure those things. It was at times like these that my own sense of disconnection receded, just a little, and I could catch a hint of my purpose.

And then one day, in the desert—where you see nothing but caravans and the brightest light is that of the sun and the stars—I saw, from a distance, a dust cloud with two bright lights speeding toward me. It was the first car that I had ever seen. I was intrigued as I looked at it and started to walk toward it, but I was about to be inspired. Destiny was calling.

SAMADHI
MEDITATION PRACTICE

Find a quiet corner, sit comfortably with a straight back and neck, and close your eyes.

Sit in silence.

Stay in this position for as long as you comfortably can.

CHAPTER 2
CHASING THE NECTAR OF IMMORTALITY

विस्मयो योगभूमिका:

The different stages of yoga cause amazement.

Until that point, my world stretched only as far as the Aravalli mountains, which I could see across the plains from the monastery where I lived. I could imagine nothing farther, wider, or greater than that. Now, a car was approaching us.

Excitement ran through our community. Who could be coming? And where could they be going? Slowly, slowly, the lights came closer and closer, and it became apparent that whoever it was, they were coming to see us.

A car was a rarity in itself, but then out of the car stepped two ladies, both with blond hair, blue eyes, and fair skin. I had never seen a Caucasian person before, and I was intrigued. One of the ladies was older, about sixty, and she introduced herself as Suzie. The younger one was perhaps fifty-five, and she introduced herself as Barbara. They were so distinctive and elegant. And they were wearing pants and shirts, something I had never seen a woman wear. My mother and my sister lived in the city, and they visited once in a while—this was common practice for the wife and family of a monk such as my father—but the monastery was primarily full of men and boys. In my life I had seen very few women, and never women like Suzie and Barbara.

The two women were just as curious about us as we were about them. It was as if they were explorers newly arrived in the Antarctic wilderness and they were seeing penguins for the very first time. I went to talk to them, and they explained that they came from a far-away land called America. They spoke to me in very simple English, and I could understand them because I had learned English from the books and comics that someone had donated to the monastery. These two ladies seemed so kind. One of them handed me a Snickers bar, another thing I had never seen before. I peeled back the wrapper and took a bite. In that moment, I tasted heaven. It was delicious, and instantly, I was hooked on the chocolate and on these divine beings who had bestowed it upon me.

As I savored this taste of heaven, Suzie and Barbara told me a story about my own land. "Here in India, there is an ancient legend about two princes in Sri Lanka," Suzie began. "The legend goes that these princes were fighting the ten-headed demon Ravana, and one of them was mortally wounded. The doctors shook their heads and said, 'The only way we can save the prince's life is if we get a special herb from the Himalayas. We have just twelve hours, and then he will die.'"

By now my eyes were round, and I was perched on the edge of my seat with excitement at this story.

"Now, the Himalayas were far, far away from Sri Lanka. This

mighty mountain range lay on the northern side of India, near China and Pakistan, and in twelve hours someone must get the herb and return to the southernmost tip of India. The only person who could achieve such a feat was the monkey god, Hanuman. And he did: Hanuman flew to the Himalayas, found this herb called Sanjeevani to heal the prince, and flew back to Sri Lanka with it. The princes returned to the fight and won the battle against the demon Ravana."

Barbara explained to me that this Sanjeevani can make you young. It can make you healthy; it can cure all ailments. According to the legend Barbara was telling me, Sanjeevani was an herb, but in our monastery we knew about Sanjeevani—not as an herb but as living energy, like *chi* (or *qi*) in traditional Chinese medicine. It is a divine energy that we create through yogic practices, and it flows from within us to create health and happiness without end.

Like two modern-day versions of Indiana Jones, Suzie and Barbara had traveled across the globe in pursuit of this herb. You might say that they were Sanjeevani chasers, determined to find the herb from the moment they heard the legend. The women went to Sri Lanka, but they couldn't find the herb there. However, they heard rumors that somewhere in the deserts of Rajasthan were secluded monasteries where the monks practice the "living Sanjeevani" arts. So, these two beautiful wise women in their shirts and pants flew thousands of miles to Sri Lanka, then thousands more miles to Rajasthan, then drove across the desert to find this fabled monastery, and finally they arrived at our doorstep.

I was both fascinated and baffled at the same time. These Sanjeevani practices were so normal to me. I had been surrounded by them all my life, like the desert sands. How did these two beings—who were to me like angels or aliens—come to be here, and what was the value of these practices that they should be chasing them across the planet? (Which apparently extended much farther than the mountain peaks that had previously marked the perimeter of my world.)

More importantly, why would Suzie and Barbara be chasing our Sanjeevani, when in my mind they already had something far more valuable: Snickers bars?

The concept of immortality is strewn throughout Eastern folklore, and it appears in many forms. There is Sanjeevani, the medicinal herb that Suzie and Barbara sought; there is *amrit*, the nectar of immortality that was churned from the oceans at the beginning of creation. Both of these are potent external substances that rejuvenate you. And then there is another concept of immortality in which you are rejuvenated not with something external but through a process called *prati prasav*. Think of the phoenix of ancient legends, which lives for hundreds of years before meeting its death in fire. Miraculously, it is reborn from the ashes to start its long life over again. In the same way, prati prasav is the process of rebirth. There is no Sanjeevani to find, no amrit to drink; instead, through prati prasav you rid yourself of all negative emotion, past pain, and lingering trauma. You are purified. In prati prasav, the dancer becomes one with the dance, and the chains that bind you to the past are broken. Through the fire of intense meditation, you are burnt to ashes and reborn in the fire, rejuvenated, peaceful, strong.

Prati prasav is a very important process that was taught to all the monks in my monastery from an early age. But imagine me as a child: How could I value prati prasav? I had no trauma, no pain. I was water from the spring, emerging pristine from the earth. Even so, I came to see that Suzie and Barbara had experienced emotions I could not even imagine, and—even if they did not know it themselves—they sought a rejuvenation that went further than skin deep.

Later, I heard Barbara and Suzie talking to my father about their quest. They were very honest with him. "We come from Los Angeles, California," Suzie explained. "My husband is a sound engineer who has worked on major movies"—she listed some films I had never heard of. "Barbara and I live in Hollywood among very famous actors and celebrities, and we have walked the red carpet like film stars ourselves. Once we were both young and beautiful, but now we are getting older, and we don't want to become old. We want this elixir, this Sanjeevani. Can you teach us?"

My father could see that their minds were running after just one thing, the pursuit of youth, and such a singular pursuit is never a healthy thing. These two women didn't know that Sanjeevani doesn't heal just the body—it can heal the mind as well. Yet even though their quest was for mere beauty, my father was more than happy to teach them. He explained to Suzie and Barbara: "Even if I give you something external, you must also go through a process of purification—prati prasav. Because as you know, you don't serve a delicious meal in an unclean bowl; you must clean the bowl first."

He described how the meditation process would take them inward so that they could let go of the past and all they were and had learned to be. Prati prasav is a guided process: it is as impossible to do on yourself as it would be to conduct surgery on your own body. Participants require a facilitator to initiate and guide them safely through the techniques. In that, it is similar to a vision quest, where a shaman will provide interpretation and guidance, or an ayahuasca ceremony with a facilitator to ensure participants are safe and supported.

"Sure," Suzie and Barbara agreed. They were ready to try.

My father had observed how intrigued I was by these women. He told them, "You will need somebody to help you do the prati prasav. This child will help you." He pointed to me.

I was a little shocked that I would be given the responsibility of taking these ladies through the process of rebirth. I'm certain that they, too, must have been shocked and maybe even annoyed because they might have expected that only the best of the best, the most senior monk, would work with them—not some child. But destiny is an interesting thing: you never know what path the guru will take to unravel your destiny for you. Now, my father had said I would be working with Suzie and Barbara. Most probably he knew I needed satsang, and that satsang sometimes comes from the most unlikely places.

Suffering occurs when we don't know ourselves. If we don't know ourselves, we create a false ego, and from that false ego come pain and sorrow, and then comes fear. If we wish to know ourselves, we must go through all the emotions that lie unresolved within us, and we must learn to let them go. Prati prasav takes us through this process until the knowledge of self—*vidya*—is achieved.

Prati prasav is a Sanksrit expression that means "reverse birthing" or "going back to the source." It is a set of yogic techniques that reconnects us with the original source of our emotions or experiences so that we can fully experience them and let them go. In this way we can release emotional blockages, trauma, and negative patterns stored in both the body and mind.

The individual elements of prati prasav are accessible to us all. They include:

Pranayama: Breathwork techniques, used to soothe the mind and body.

Meditation: Focusing the mind on a single point, such as the breath, a mantra, or an image, to cultivate inner peace and clarity.

Yoga asanas: Movements and flows to release emotions and blockages in the body and stimulate the flow of energy.

Simple the practices may be, but prati prasav can unfold over your entire lifetime as you explore it more and more deeply. That would certainly prove to be true in my own life.

Starting this process with Suzie and Barbara, I experienced the kind of pain I had seen only in the animals I cared for; I did not know humans could suffer in this manner. All my life I had seen just the ecstasy of the monk, and now for the first time I was exploring the other side of the emotional spectrum. The things that were so easy for me—taking a deep breath, inhaling, going deep within, witnessing the dancer—I saw how hard it could be for a normal person.

Each of our sessions started with a spark that stirred and grew until there was a raging fire. Slowly the fire died down until there was nothing but ash. Each day, Suzie and Barbara released their emotions, and by the end of the day, they were filled with peace and calm.

As the two women opened their hearts during the meditations, I started to realize a different aspect of the world. Some of their emotions were too complex for me to understand, but it wasn't my place to understand what was going on inside them. My job was as a guide, to take them to an inner destination and help them overcome whatever it was that they were feeling. But I distinctly remember the gratitude and contentment that I could see on their faces after each session.

Barbara and Suzie joined us at the monastery for seven days. They sat and they meditated, and the process of prati prasav unfolded. They wanted more, so they decided to stay another seven days. Then they delayed their departure for another week and another, until finally they stayed with us for four weeks.

In that month, the women changed. In the first week, they were still oriented toward the world, and they wanted to go back and conquer it with this ancient secret knowledge. In the second week, their perspective changed, and they could see the absurdities in their quest. By the third week, they had become more stoic, more spiritual, more divine. And by the fourth week, they were reborn.

They had stopped seeing me as a child, and I had stopped seeing them as outsiders. They were working as intently and intensely as any senior monk. When they first arrived, Barbara and Suzie were like two tourists in Times Square, gawking and walking backward and getting in the way of the crowds surging around them. They didn't know their place or their purpose. If you have ever driven in an Indian city, you will know that it looks like chaos, but everyone has a purpose: this is why the vehicles flow around each other and no one crashes into anyone else. After four weeks, Suzie and Barbara had found their place. They had indeed found the Sanjeevani they were seeking, which is the divine energy of immortality.

All my short life I had heard about the different processes of immortality, but I'd never seen people change in such a manner. When the monks meditated, they were already in a higher place, and they remained in a high place, without a discernible difference. When you water a pot holding a blossoming plant with glossy green leaves, you won't see much difference. But imagine if the pot contains nothing but a seed, and you water it, and the most beautiful flower starts to grow. Every day I saw Suzie and Barbara change, and as they changed something inside me changed too.

In those four weeks I was also absorbing their stories of the world, how vast and complicated it is. When they told me their stories, it was not like listening to fairy tales. It was like watching a movie with the director's commentary because it was clear they had so much wisdom about the world. They told me all about America, about its wonders and marvels like fast food and technology. Many years later, when I came to America, it was not as if I was coming to a completely new place because I had learned so many things from Suzie and Barbara.

After meeting Suzie and Barbara, I became curious about the outside world, and that was something new for me. In the monastery, there's this idea that the people outside the monastery walls are very different from us, almost another species. Now I saw that we were not so different after all; we all have access to the divine immortality within ourselves, though many do not know it. Not only that, but I also saw that people can evolve. From those weeks with Suzie and Barbara, I discovered that this knowledge we had, this divine energy, this Sanjeevani—immortality—could truly change people. When those two women arrived, they were suffering; when they left, they were full of joy.

I am sure it surprised them at first to find that immortality is not found in the form of an herb or a guru—or fame, riches, and the applause of a crowd. Instead, they found that each of us can cultivate immortality inside ourselves. It is cultivated through actions as simple as the samadhi practices in this book. We have untapped potential to not only enjoy, but also to *create* good health, success, happiness, and positivity.

Suzie and Barbara said they came to the monastery looking for youth and beauty, but they were really seeking the joy and confidence that came with being young and beautiful. They may not have found the herbal equivalent of the fountain of youth that they were seeking, but they left with a deeper sense of contentedness and a means of finding their way back to that feeling within themselves, anytime and anywhere.

Before these two women arrived, I had been wondering what my purpose was. Now I pondered: What if my purpose was to help other people? Inspired, I started imagining a fairy tale of my own. Now I would teach people the divine protocols, and they would treat me like a hero too. I didn't know about Thor or Superman, but I started to think that one day I would be like Hanuman, the monkey god, who flew the Sanjeevani from the Himalayas to the battlefield in Sri Lanka and became a hero. I would go around the world finding Suzies and Barbaras and share the divine energy of Sanjeevani with them. They would get healed, and they would be so happy and appreciative of me. I really liked this fairy tale.

It seemed to me a very reasonable goal—but then, I really knew very little about people. When you are a monk, people don't talk to you like a normal person. They see you as either a healer or an oddity. If the locals approach you, it is with questions about how you can help them. Or bizarre questions: Can you fly? Do you fart rainbows? They hardly see us as human. The other young monks are on their own spiritual path, absorbed with their journey of reaching their inner selves. The elder monks are on a higher level, so you don't talk to them in a human way either, asking: What did you eat? How did you sleep? No, you don't do chitchat with them. You are told to revere them and to speak to them only if it's truly necessary, so you don't waste their energies, which are as precious as gold. My father was the head monk, so he was out of reach, and my mother and my sister lived in the city and were also out of reach in a different way.

Suzie and Barbara showed me there was another way to interact with humans and with the world. They were not the elder monks, on a higher plane that was so far out of reach, nor were they like my peers, who were so preoccupied that they didn't seek to make the kind of connection that I had made with Suzie and Barbara. Before these two women came to the monastery, I didn't know or care about the outside world. After they left, I started to care because I had a different perspective. I could see that people outside my little world were not so different from me, and I had something that might be valuable to them.

Now it seemed to me that there are only two kinds of people: the ones who have already realized the god within, and the ones who have the potential to realize the god within. I knew there was something more for me to do. I could meditate and I would get happiness for myself, but if I could help somebody else achieve that state, the happiness that would give me would be beyond compare. Suzie and Barbara showed me what it was like to be a teacher as well as a student, and I was captivated.

For the first time in my life, I was not simply intrigued, but inspired. I had a reason to learn everything that my master was teaching me. I had an agenda of mastering immortality because I wanted to be the Hanuman who would take the Sanjeevani to the ones who needed it.

More and more, I started to pursue the outside world. I wanted to be in that vast world, not the small one I had always known—even though my own small world contained everything I would ever need. I just didn't know it yet.

When you receive the gift of immortality, there is freedom from pain and suffering, and there is real joy—the kind of joy that cannot be snatched away from you, because it comes from within. The benefits of prati prasav extend well beyond a feeling of yogic calm: when you cultivate this inner rejuvenation, you are not wasting time worrying that you will not have enough. You are coming from a place of plenty rather than a place of lack.

Most of us are like a shaken-up Coke bottle, ready to explode. So first we must calm ourselves: in our bodies, our breath, and our minds. Only then can we know what it is that we seek.

SAMADHI MEDITATION PRACTICE

Sit quietly and close your eyes.
Observe your body.
Feel whatever arises, and continue for as long as you can.

CHAPTER 3
BECOMING A MASTER OF TIME

**गुरु गोविन्द दोउ खड़े, काकेलागूँ पाय ;
बलिहारी गुरु आपने, गोविन्द दियो बताये।**

*If my guru and God are both in front of me, who will I salute first?
It must be my guru, as only by his teaching am I able to see God.*

A child who lives immersed in nature is deeply aware of the environment that is around them. Every day of my childhood, I would look up at the sky and I would see the sun. Now, the setting sun and the rising sun are both orange, so if you are sitting and get lost in your thoughts and meditations, sometimes you may look up at that sun as it nears the horizon and wonder, *Is it the beginning of the day or is it the end?* You do not know because the start and the finish are so similar.

The orange sun marked two of the most beautiful times for me during the day. When the sun is rising it is called the *Brahma muhurta*, meaning God's time. And when the sun is setting, it is called *Sandhya kala*: again, it is God's time. During the day you follow your schedule and do whatever it is you are supposed to be doing, but these two specific times at the beginning and the end are the most important in the life of a spiritual seeker. As a young monk, this was the time I would spend with my father. Then I would have my lessons with him, and Babaji would be teaching me, working on me, molding me, carving me. He was the orange sun, and I was the orange sun beneath the orange sun.

By this time in my life, even though I was still very young—no more than ten years old—much purification had already taken place within me because, just as I had done prati prasav with Suzie and Barbara, I had done many cycles of prati prasav myself. When the mind starts to purify, then every thought is very powerful. I remember one of my teachers telling me the story of how Isaac Newton was sitting under a tree when an apple fell and hit his head. This very simple event led him to think about gravity. Now, I do not know if the story is true or not, but if it is, imagine that something so mundane as an apple falling on somebody's head can change the course of physics. It wasn't just Isaac Newton: James Watt was inspired to redesign the steam engine by watching a kettle boiling. Before Newton, many apples had fallen, and before Watt, many kettles had boiled, yet each prior incident had been like a single wave in a chaotic ocean—lost in the multitude. But if the ocean is calm and there is just a single wave, imagine how much influence that one wave could have.

The same happened with me; Suzie and Barbara were the apple falling on my head. Visitors come along and it is not so unusual: visitors come and apples fall all the time. You walk on the road and bump into people, and these events are of no particular value. But this one occasion was, for me, my singular apple that changed everything.

Babaji could see that I had changed. So that day as I sat in front of him underneath the orange sun during the Brahma muhurta, he told me to meditate on the nature of the world.

"I want you to meditate on the fact that we are born to die, and we die to be born again," he told me. "The cycle of birth and death in which the individual is caught is *samsara*, and this cycle will last as long as ignorance lasts. As a student, you must let go of ignorance and meditate on the truth."

I looked at him, puzzled. "What kind of ignorance do you mean?"

There are three forms of ignorance, Babaji explained to me. "Firstly, ignorance could be *moh*, the ignorance of attachment. If we yearn after a fine car or fancy clothes so that people will think well of us, that is moh. If we chase after the approval of a friend, that too is moh."

"After moh there is *bandha*, meaning bondage," he went on. "This is a state of being bound or tied down by worldly attachments, desires, and ignorance. Bandha makes you feel trapped in a place, a situation, a circumstance. In this bondage, you can never be free."

And finally, he talked about *maya*. "Maya is the illusion created by perceptions and appearances that veil the true nature of the world. We overcome maya when we come to recognize the unity of all existence."

I was confused. "But isn't the world just... the world?"

"Think about it like this," my father said. "Light falls on a tree, and that light is perceived by your eyes. This causes an electrical impulse, which is received by your brain, creating an image in your mind. The tree in front of you is separate from the image of the tree that is created in your mind. Not only that, you may choose to interpret it as a beautiful tree or an ugly tree, a healthy tree or an unhealthy tree. The marvel in all of this is that the tree remains unaffected by your interpretations. The tree is what the tree is, the tree is the truth. And it is only you who is living with that particular interpretation of the truth. Each person has their own unique interpretation of the world that they create in their own head. And that world is maya."

Babaji explained to me: "As a student, if you are caught in this samsara, you must free yourself, and to free yourself you must go beyond the bondages, the attachments and illusions."

I gazed at him, digesting all of this. "Where do these attachments and illusions come from?"

"If a child is not given access to truth and knowledge, there is delusion," he replied. "If there is no light, there is darkness. You see, there are three main delusions a spiritual seeker must overcome," Babaji said, holding up one finger. "The first is *I am this body*. With this delusion comes attachment to the body. I am man, I am woman; I'm pretty, I'm ugly. There comes pain or joy, and both are irrelevant because the body is constantly changing. A person who believes *I am this body* will always be in a state of chaos."

Babaji held up a second finger. "The second delusion is *What is in front of me is the only truth*. What I see, what I observe is the only truth. This delusion does not allow a person to go in search of samadhi, the infinite."

"Tell me about this samadhi," I asked him.

"Samadhi means you are a master of time, where each second is worth a million years and a million years is worth a second," my father explained. "Time has no meaning, no dominion over us. There is only peace, and if you can achieve that peace, then you are one with the immortal consciousness. You are no longer limited by perceived boundaries, so the things you can accomplish become limitless. In the state of samadhi, you are one with the universal consciousness."

Babaji held up a third finger. "And the third delusion is *The objective of my life is to fulfill my senses*. The sensations of our eyes, ears, nose, mouth, and skin. This delusion tells me that my purpose is just to run after delicious food, pretty things, nice music, good smells, the touch and the warmth of another person. If I run around bound by this delusion, then it is a cycle that will never end. To let go of these delusions, we must meditate on the truth." He lowered his hand and gazed at me, waiting for my next question.

"What is the truth?" I asked him then.

"You are the infinite. You come from the infinite, and you will go to the infinite. Visualize yourself as if you are not *part* of the universe; you *are* the universe. Do not think of the drop separate from the ocean. When you sit and meditate, try to create the visualization that the drop has become one with the ocean. Say to yourself, *I am one with the universe. I am one with the light.*"

He told me to meditate on this, and as I did, I kept on thinking about what he had told me. My eyes were closed, there was a peaceful bliss on my face, my muscles were relaxed—but inside me, one thought was jumping around.

When Babaji said, "Ignorance is just accepting what is in front of you," was I being ignorant by being content with just being in the monastery? What about the world that I had experienced through Suzie and Barbara? I had seen them change; I'd seen them overcome the attachments, the bondages, the illusions. And I'd seen them overcome this samsara and go toward *sakshatkar*—realization, enlightenment, experiencing the divine. No longer were they limited by their belief that youth and beauty were the greatest goal. What if there were more Suzies and Barbaras in this world? What if just like Babaji was helping me and I helped those two women, there were more that could be helped? What other stories lay in this world?

In the monastery, I knew some monks were adamant that the path to enlightenment lay in seclusion: separating oneself from the temptations and distractions of this world. Others were sure that enlightenment was achieved by submitting to the pressures of this world and emerging awakened.

As I sat there, I couldn't stop thinking about this dilemma. The beautiful thing is one cannot lie to one's teacher. I knew Babaji observed me, and—master that he was—he saw through me. He could see every thought, every emotion, every twitch. And I knew that he knew what I was thinking. I was a bit afraid, for he was telling me to rise up. And I was rising toward the world.

I thought that when I opened my eyes from the meditation, he might not be happy with me, but when I opened my eyes, I saw that he was smiling.

"Why do you smile, Babaji?" I asked him.

"Your curiosity reminds me of myself when I was young," he replied.

"Tell me the story," I asked him. "How did you come to this monastery? How did your journey begin?"

Suddenly, I saw him change a little bit. From the guru, he became the father. He lifted me and put me in his lap. Resting his hand on my head, he began to tell me his story.

"I was born in the world of Suzie and Barbara, in a time that was very chaotic. My family comes from an ancient lineage that had accumulated generational wealth, culture, and wisdom. My parents were well off, very settled, content with their lives. But it was a time of war. India is a great country, and it was a vast country. And India suffered occupation, and the colonials had little knowledge or understanding of this country and its cultures and its people. In 1947, they drew a line and split India into two nations: Hindu-majority India and Muslim-majority Pakistan. Suddenly, the people who had lived in this great land, whose ancestors had lived in this great land, were told that where they live is not their country anymore; they must be part of an exodus. It was one of the largest mass migrations in human history and came with violence on a scale that had seldom been seen before. Fourteen million refugees moved from one nation to another, believing they would return one day and so taking nothing of value with them.

"Among them, my parents fled to the Dominion of India, leaving everything they owned behind. My family saw great suffering, misery, chaos, death, and destruction as they came to their new home, the nation that was created. But they left behind in their old home everything that they had, all their inheritance created by generations. My family had enjoyed exorbitant wealth: they had servants, money, and luxury of every kind. And now they were paupers with nothing to their name. My father could not recover from the shock of loss. A few years after partition, he left his body, leaving behind my mother with her eight children."

My father looked at me and smiled sadly, as he tried to explain to me what he had experienced. Maybe he was a good father because he had been a child—maybe five, six years old—when he lost his father. He was trying to explain to me what it is like for a child to lose their father—how the world changes overnight, how innocence goes away, how the cycles of samsara continue, how the people who are living must push through, push forward, and how absolute that is.

I listened to him intently. I had not thought that my father had experienced such emotions, for when I saw him, he was always perfect, divine, graceful, dignified, powerful. And even as he explained these terrible events to me, there was a calmness on his face. It was my eyes that widened as I started to think what that loss would be like. How remarkable it is that for something that's so certain to touch everybody's lives, we never talk about death.

My father continued. "Life was very tough after my father died. We learned how it felt to be hungry. Even so, because I was so young, poverty was entirely normal to me. I wasn't born from plenty—I was born from the dirt that surrounded us. I had never seen luxury; I had never possessed riches. So our existence did not seem like hardship at all. In that household darkened by sorrow, I was the happiest being. As I grew, I couldn't understand why everyone else in the house was depressed. I made the best of what I had, even though it wasn't much.

"Even so, as I grew in understanding, I could see that the world was divided into haves and have nots, and that I was on the less fortunate side of the divide. Once I asked my mother, 'Why don't I have any toys like the other children? How come there are some children at school who are not always hungry?'

"'That is because they have a father, and you don't,' my mother told me.

"Then I realized that life isn't the same for everyone. The only consolation I had was my eldest brother. I loved him dearly, and he cared for me as best as he could. After our father died, my brother took the role of patriarch, providing stability and working to support our family as best he could. When I was eight years old, my brother became very sick. The doctors in India at that time were limited in their resources. They told my mother, 'We cannot help the child; he will die. Take him home, spend as much time as you can with him, and prepare for his death.' My mother, who had lost her husband a few years back, now prepared herself to lose her son."

As I gazed up at my father's face, I imagined what it would be like to be in a house with a loved one, waiting for their death. What would the emotion be, when faced with such a thought? Does one accept one's fate? Or does one want to challenge it? And even if one wants to challenge it, with what? What means, resources, or knowledge do we have to challenge our fate?

It was as if my father knew what I was thinking. "When my brother was sick, I realized how very absolute death is, how very permanent it is. I was only a child, and I had nothing but prayer in my arsenal of desperation."

My father smiled again as he looked at me. "Each day I would look up at the sky, and I would see the orange sun. And I would call out to the sun, 'If there is anybody listening, help me. Save my brother.' Over and over again, I called out, 'Please show me the way.' I prayed with all the passion an eight-year-old child can muster. Such desperation can only come out of love. It is the desperation of a mother whose infant is sick, and she will do anything to save them, or a father whose children are hungry, and he will strike any bargain to feed them. I was ready to do anything to save my brother, but I didn't know what.

"Then one day, my desperate prayers were answered. At that moment, when I was at my most vulnerable, there was a knock on the door. An old man stood on our doorstep. He was ancient, and yet he radiated power. You see, in that region, at that time, there were monks who would go door-to-door begging for food. And this monk came to our house and said, 'I am hungry.' In our house there was a tradition that remained from the time when our family had plenty. It was that all saints must be respected, and all who are hungry must be fed. My mother looked through the kitchen to find something from whatever little we had. She went out to the monk at the door, carrying a small bundle of food for him. The monk looked at my mother, whose face was filled with sorrow and misery. 'Amah, why are you sad? Why do you cry?' he asked. My mother replied, 'I have a sick son in my house, and doctors say he will die.' The man smiled. And he said, 'You are giving me food, so let me try to help you. Take me to the child.'

"My mother took this beggar, this saint, to the room where my brother lay, sick and dying. And the saint said, 'Can I have some time with the child alone?' My mother left the room, leaving me in there. Nobody thought to look in the corner where I sat, silently observing like a fly on the wall. Insignificant, not knowing that this incident would change my life forever.

"As I watched, I saw the monk change. From him came a flash of light, so bright that it melted away all forms—just like a flame melts the wax on a candle. No matter how much I squinted against that light, I could not open my eyes fully. In that light, the forms started to fade, and then everything in the room started to dissolve and become light—the table, the chair, the fan, the ceiling—until all that remained floating in that light was the monk and my brother. And then suddenly, the light started to become even brighter, and the monk, too, became nothing but pure light. In that light, now, only my brother remained. Slowly, I saw my brother, too, fading away until only light remained, nothing else. Then, in that light I could see a form appearing. And in that form, I saw my brother once again, but this time he was different, somehow. Then from that light, the form of the monk came back, too. The room, the chair, the table, the fan came back, and the light retreated back to the heart of the monk.

"Instantly my brother woke up, as if from a deep sleep. 'I'm hungry,' he said. 'Where's my mother?'

"The monk called the rest of the family back inside, and everyone was so excited, elated, jumping with joy to see the boy, who had been trembling with a deathly fever just minutes before, suddenly looking not pale, but healthy and stout. My mother just accepted the miracle for what it was, for she had been hurt by life too much to question whatever grace was bestowed upon her.

"And as my family was rejoicing I knew, child that I was, that I had found something of immense value. While my family was gathered around my brother, the monk started to leave. I ran to him and asked his name. 'My name is Swami Jagannath,' the monk replied, which literally means 'master of the universe.' 'I am the last living member of the ancient lineage of Shiv Yogis.'

"I replied, 'If you are the master of the universe, then you are my master too. I pray to you, teach me. Teach me the truth. Teach me this freedom. Teach me what you did. Teach me the ways of light. I saw so much pain and fear inside me, and then I saw you. And within a moment, the pain and fear were gone. Take me as your disciple, so I can learn to do what you just did.'

"Until then I had felt helpless, unable to rescue the people I loved. Now in this monk I saw power. Most importantly, I saw that this power would enable me never to be helpless and afraid again.

"If a child goes to a pilot and says, 'I want to learn how to fly,' you can imagine that the pilot will want to teach them. It's natural to respond to that desire. But there is something even more about these great yogis, these enlightened masters, these liberated ones. There is a saying that a liberated person is the one who is established as a ruler of energy. A liberated person is a source of wisdom—not just in spiritual matters, but also in how to live our life. Most importantly, a liberated person is somebody who can connect to your feelings and emotions. They can see into your eyes, right into your soul. What I did not know then was that in my curiosity and my eagerness, I had passed a great test. Jagannath could see that, even at such a young age, I had been primed by faith, chiseled by everything that life had thrown at me. Jagannath knew I would fulfill every instruction, climb every mountain, and be the best of the Shiv Yogis.

"So Jagannath looked at me and saw the curiosity, the hunger, inside me. 'I will take you and I will teach you,' he said.

"Jagannath went to my mother and asked if he could take this young child under his wing. And my mother, probably overwhelmed by all the other mouths she had to feed, said, 'Sure. I give you responsibility for this boy; I make you his ward. Take him, teach him. Make him what you will.' And that was when my journey started."

I sat there, astonished. I thought my father was born a monk. I thought he just manifested in the center of the universe, completely the way he was, just like a grape appears on a vine or a mango on a tree! Who would have thought that all monks have a journey to become what they are? Because I was born in this place, this was the only world I knew. But my father had come from somewhere else, the world of Suzie and Barbara. Jagannath, this great monk, had held his hand and given him mercy and compassion. This one event changed my father irrevocably. But not just him; it changed my life as well. That day Jagannath was destined to meet my father. Jagannath was the orange sun that was setting. And my father was the orange sun that was rising, a new destiny that was being created.

After listening to Babaji's story and hearing of the mercy Jagannath had bestowed upon him, my mind was made up. If Jagannath could go out into the world—a world I had glimpsed in my talks with Suzie and Barbara—and find my father, then maybe I, too, could go out. Maybe my attachment to being in the monastery was the bondage I must overcome.

But then I wondered, *Or maybe this is an illusion being created by my mind?* As I listened to my father, I had two very powerful thoughts inside me. One thought was that *I am home, I am content.* And the other thought was *Be Jagannath, be the master of the world—go out.* And I did not know which thought to follow.

And at that time, young child that I was, I was wondering, *Which orange sun am I? Am I the orange sun setting into a meditative place of realization? Or am I the orange sun rising up to fulfill a mission?*

As I sat there, puzzling over the paths that lay before me, a crow flew over my head. I looked up and saw that it had a fish in its mouth, and three or four other crows were hurtling after it, in hot pursuit of its prize. The crow's life was in danger, but it flew on, stubbornly refusing to drop the fish. I wanted to cry out, "Just let it go!" But then I thought, *Maybe humans are just like that crow: hanging on to something we think is so valuable, refusing to see the danger this attachment is bringing to us, limited by our self-imposed boundaries.* Suddenly, it seemed that illusion, attachment, and bondage were everywhere to be seen. If we could only let go of our conscious thinking and enter the space between thoughts, only then could we shake off our ignorances and delusions and find freedom.

But that idea could wait. Now it was time to start my day and practice samadhi.

SAMADHI MEDITATION PRACTICE

Close your eyes and gently shift your awareness from your head to your heart, and then to your navel, knees, and down to your toes.

Slowly bring your awareness back up from your toes to the top of your head.

Repeat this process three times.

CHAPTER 4

CONNECTING TO THE IMMORTAL SELF

अभिलाषाद् बहिर्गतिः संवाह्यस्य

*Due to desire moving outward for external objects,
an individual is carried from life to life.*

In a secluded corner of the monastery that not many people knew about, a few of us children found a magnificent and ancient mango tree. We were delighted because we knew that there was one time during the year when the tree would bear delicious, juicy, huge mangoes.

When the mangoes first appear, they are green and sour. Then they start to become yellowish, but even now they are not so good to eat. In the summertime, when they turn reddish yellow, then is the perfect time to eat those mangoes. Even the greediest child learns to wait just one more day for perfection.

Every day through summer, all of us kids would visit the tree to see if the fruit was ripe yet. It was irresistible to us: something secret, a little forbidden, involving delicious, sweet, edible treats. Standing there, we would speculate about the revered monks of the monastery who might have visited that exact same tree through the years.

"Maybe Baba Gorakhnath came here?" one boy mused.

"Yes, or Jagannath?" responded another.

"Even Shivanand!" a third whispered in awe. It blew our young minds, thinking about our saints being naughty little kids themselves, coming to eat the mangoes of that ancient tree.

As we anticipated our own mango feast, we giggled with excitement. This would not be an American feast, where you can eat some and put the rest in the refrigerator for later. No, this would be a monastic feast. We couldn't go back with the evidence that we had been eating mangoes during our free time. This had to be a one-stop feast, a single mammoth meal, one and done.

The mangoes themselves delighted me, of course, but also the notion of seasons intrigued me. I contemplated the idea that there is always a time for everything and, no matter how much I want the mangoes throughout the year, no matter how much I pray for ripe mangoes, there is always a time for the mangoes to emerge. I had become wise enough to know that even when I could see a mango hanging in the tree, there would be a time to pluck the mango and a time to eat the mango.

For example, if I went to the tree before its season, there would be no mangoes. And then if I saw a mango and plucked it before it was ripe, the mango would be sour. So I always had to respect time, be aware of time, and wait for the right time. As I stood before that tree, I could see, if I waited patiently, that the time to eat those mangoes was coming.

Frankly, I did not care all that much how this tree came to exist there, how old it was, or who planted it. All I needed to know was that every year during the summer months, this tree would become important to me.

A young monk such as myself would see time in a very particular way. In the monastery there were various buildings that we visited regularly. There was Annapoorneshwari Hall—named for the god of food—where we were fed. You wouldn't think about the hall until it was the right time to go there, when there was food to be eaten. There was the meditation hall; it was always there, but we knew what time to go there to receive our instruction. There was the prayer temple, and we knew to go there at the right time for prayer.

We children were very aware of time. We tracked it through the position of the sun, so we would keep a watch on the sun over the course of a day. We would listen carefully to the songs of the birds, and we knew which birds indicated the crack of dawn and which birds sang the sweet lullaby of the night. Even through the frenzied activity of the ants, we knew when the seasons were changing and when we could expect rains.

As I walked through the monastery, I would look around this beautiful complex, and I would sometimes wonder, *Where does it all come from?* Because just like the seasons affect the mango tree, so that I got mangoes once a year, I understood that everything has its own chronology. There are flowers that are born and die in a week. There are birds that have a lifespan of a few years, and there are insects who live for just one day. I wondered, *What is the lifespan of this monastery?* For I knew that it had already endured for many, many centuries.

As I pondered these questions, I reached the very center of the monastery, where the prayer temple lay. This building was considered the oldest part of the monastery and its heart, like the sun at the center of the solar system. Inside that temple there were three cylindrical structures of great spiritual significance, called *shivlings*. This term is derived from two Sanskrit words: *Shiva*, referring to Lord Shiva, and *linga*, which means "mark" or "sign." Shivlings occupy a very sacred place in my tradition. They speak to us of the principles of creation and destruction, represent the universal consciousness in a physical form, and signify the divine energy and creative power of Lord Shiva.

All gods are intricate beings, difficult for our mortal minds to comprehend, but Shiva in particular is spoken of as having many faces. He is the destroyer, slayer of demons; but he is also a husband and father. Not only that, he is the supreme lord who creates, protects, and transforms the universe. So, too, the shivlings represent these different aspects of Lord Shiva. When we pray before the shivlings, we are encouraged to look beyond external forms and connect with the inner essence of divinity within ourselves.

Each of these three cylindrical structures was made of a different precious stone or metal. First was the *parad shivling*, made of mercury—considered a sacred metal, associated with healing and spiritual transformation and purified through many alchemical processes. This shivling signifies creation. When something is born, it is beautiful, and it is through the grace of the universe a new thing has come into being. Second was the *narmadeshwar shivling*, a stone of a unique shape that is found on the banks of the River Narmada and then covered in silver. It signifies maintenance, by which I mean the period between birth and death. Anything that is born has a lifespan, and the narmadeshwar signifies that existence. And last was the *sphatik shivling*: crafted from a single piece of quartz crystal, it signifies death. Together, there are birth, life, and death. My father had explained that we monks have to master all three shivlings: the creation, the maintenance, and death.

When we would meditate inside the temple, my father taught me that a fourth shivling also exists. You can't see this fourth shivling because it is a *jyotirlinga*: a shivling made up of light. "That is the shivling every yogi must master," he told me, "because it signifies the evolution that comes after death. The acceptance, the peace, and the start of a new cycle. If this fourth shivling is not mastered, we do not embrace destruction—instead we deny it. We crave to go back to the way things were: to stop the flow of time, not to master it. The people who deny destruction become terribly sad; they are stuck, wishing for a life that will never return."

These are very abstract concepts for a child to grasp, so then Babaji told me the story with which the Bhagavad Gita, the great Hindu scripture, begins.

Arjuna, a prince who has endured years of exile, is driven by a desire for justice against those who have wronged his family. Through all those years in exile he has trained so that when he has the opportunity in war, he can defeat his enemies and finally have justice for himself and his family. At last, on the battlefield of Kurukshetra, the armies face each other, and Arjuna finds himself facing his kin, for those who wronged him were part of his own family. Riding on his chariot, Arjuna is overwhelmed with doubt and turmoil. His resolve falters; his knees weaken. He trembles with anxiety, and his bow slips from his grasp.

As luck would have it, Vishnu himself is serving as Arjuna's charioteer. Alongside Shiva and Brahma, Vishnu is one of the three great gods. Now, he appears in the incarnation of Krishna. In his moment of crisis, Arjuna confides in Vishnu-as-Krishna. "I am not ready for this! I cannot lift an arrow against my own teachers, my uncles, my cousins. What is the point of this destruction?"

Arjuna is torn: part of him knows that the conflict is justified, while another part just wants to run away and avoid the suffering that will come.

Thus begins Krishna's teaching in the Bhagavad Gita, aimed at enlightening Arjuna so that he realizes the transient nature of this life. Krishna explains to Arjuna that once he understands the temporary nature of the body, he can learn to connect to the eternal soul, the eternal being: the fourth shivling. Only then will he be able to perform his duty (dharma) without attachment, instead of acting out of selfish desires (karma). For to every action there is an equal and opposite reaction. If we are motivated by our vices, our lusts, our anger, and our unresolved emotions, we will perpetuate our suffering and bondage, leading to ever more misery. But once we know the real nature of the self, whatever actions we perform will be the dharma—actions rooted in truth and duty—that help the flow of life itself and lead to spiritual liberation.

Through Krishna's wisdom, Arjuna is encouraged to embrace his role in upholding dharma, despite the anguish that accompanies it.

To this day, scholars and philosophers ponder why Krishna, the God of gods in all his wisdom and power, did not simply prevent the war. Some argue that war was necessary for the transition from the age of divine kingship to a time of human equality and free will. This shift, though tumultuous, ushered in a new era where individuals are responsible for their actions and choices, shaping the course of the world.

This tale of Arjuna is one that every father tells his children, just as Babaji was telling it to me now. "Arjuna knew what he had to do, but he wanted to run away from it," he said to me. "Krishna showed him that even he could not run from the inevitable forever. It was time to stop running and surrender."

It is the same for all of us, my father explained. All of us must let go of our desires: it is just a matter of time. One of these days we will have to let go, whether it is old age, dementia, or death that loosens our fingers. We can choose to let go today—but it is only possible if we connect to that bird on the upper branch, our immortal self.

Sitting before my father in the prayer temple, though, my brow wrinkled in puzzlement. "But am I not just my body? I know it is real. I can feel it! But I cannot feel my soul."

Babaji nodded. "There was a fellow called Kakbhushundi who thought the very same thing," he replied. And he went on to tell me this story.

When Kakbhushundi went to the great sage Agastya to learn, he kept asking the same question over and over again. He could not understand that he was not his body, he was an eternal being. Agastya gave him the same answers, over and over again. Finally, when Kakhbushundi asked the same question one more time, Agastya lost his patience and cursed him to be a crow.

The crow has just one word: "Kya!" In Hindi, *kya* means "what." So the crow keeps saying, "What? What? What?"

His master thought it was entirely appropriate that Kakhbushundi, with his never-ending questions, was condemned to an eternity of asking, "What?"

Yet the moment Kakhbushundi became a crow, all truth was revealed to him. He had been so connected to his physical body, he couldn't imagine anything more than that. Now he was physically a crow, yet he still had his consciousness. Suddenly, it made sense to him: "Of course I am the soul! Because if I were my body, how could I now be a crow?"

Cursed though he was to live as a crow, the curse helped Kakhbushundi to shake off the limitations of the body and connect to his immortal self.

My mind buzzing with so many new ideas, I left my father to set about my daily chores. As I worked, I pondered the cycle of birth, maintenance, and death that the shivlings represented in the monastery. This cycle was no abstract notion to us monks. Our job was to maintain this place, and just as each part of the human body has its role to play, so the monks did too. Some were the red blood cells, carrying nutrients through the body. Some monks were the brains, giving guidance. Some were the liver, providing cleansing. There were even some who were given the job of the anus: to clean out the cows' manure. We young monks were the nerve cells, running here and there with information, resources, and supplies, so all of the parts could work together harmoniously.

No matter our individual roles, all of us knew that one of our great purposes in life was to make sure that which was created by the ancient masters remained strong and steady. By maintaining that eternal legacy, the present and the future generations could be inspired.

It is said that thousands of years ago, the first guru, Adinath, meditated at this very place. And in front of the three shivlings, he mastered the fourth, the jyotirlinga, representing the evolution that comes after death. As Adinath meditated, his knowledge, his wisdom, his understanding of the universe and the patterns in the universe grew phenomenally, and many devotees came to him.

The legend spread that a wise man who had the knowledge to dispel all darkness lived in the Aravalli mountains. Many saints came to receive this knowledge from him, and they too meditated and mastered the three visible shivlings and the fourth jyotirling.

As each of these successors became enlightened, they added new aspects to the monastery. For example, I was told that the hall where we all came together to eat was established at least five generations ago by one of the great monks called Bade Baba. And in the place where we meditated, Baba Gorakhnath placed the foundation rock almost eight generations ago. Each time a new generation arose, they would maintain the old forms that already existed, and they would add some new flavor, some new beautification—something that made this place even more vibrant.

Adinath and his followers were the Krishnas to the Arjunas who would come after, bringing them enlightenment. In India, we say *Jyot se jyot jalao*, meaning "Let your lamp light my lamp." By this we mean that the one who has seen the truth and knows their real self, the eternal self, is the one who can help guide people who are stuck in misery. The one who is beyond the quicksand is the one who can help someone who is sinking. This is the immortal legacy of the divine beings or saints, which continues from Adinath: they are the light that helps others who are stuck in the darkness. For think of what would have happened if there were no Krishna for Arjuna.

This eternal legacy (we call it *sanatana parampara*) is like a constant fountain, a stream that is always flowing. If anybody is ever thirsty, he goes to the stream to drink the water. They say that the Sahara Desert used to be an ocean, but it isn't an ocean anymore—so how will I get water there? Adinath made sure that the stream is continuous, an immortal legacy that keeps flowing. So if there is ever an Arjuna who is in doubt or despair, he can go to that stream and quench his thirst.

Just as Lord Shiva has many faces, so too does immortality. One of them is this handing down of wisdom from generation to generation so the stream never runs dry. This face of immortality is one that we can all play a part in.

As I pondered about the intertwining of permanence and evolution, I walked into the meditation hall. This was a powerful place for me because it showed the lineage of the great monks, the great immortals. Some were represented with paintings, others with statues. For the really ancient ones, there were just names scribbled in stone. These were the ones whom I loved imagining. What would their strength be? How would they sit and meditate?

I would get very excited, thinking that these ancient powers had once walked in this same hall. They would have stood underneath these same stone arches. They would have meditated sitting on the same corner where I sat today, maybe sharing the same seat with the great monks who came before them. One day I, too, would master the jyotirling, attaining spiritual liberation as I was freed from the cycle of birth, life, and death. I, too, would not fear destruction, knowing that I was more than the limitations of this physical body.

SAMADHI MEDITATION PRACTICE

Sit comfortably and close your eyes.
Relax your body and observe your thoughts in silence.

CHAPTER 5
FROM DESTRUCTION, A SEED GROWS

जातस्य हि ध्रुवो मृत्युर् ध्रुवं जन्म मृतस्य च
तस्माद् अपरिहार्येऽर्थे न त्वां शोचितुम् अर्हसि

For one who has been born, death is certain; and for one who has died, birth is certain. Therefore, do not lament the inevitable.

When all of the monks were gathered in the meditation hall one day, my father came in, dressed in white. He addressed us all. "Today will be a special meditation," he told us. Babaji looked directly at me, smiled, and said, "Today, the meditation that we are going to do is the *antim yatra*, which means 'the final journey.'"

In some remarkable way, he seemed to have connected to the thoughts that had been occupying my mind: about the cycle of birth, life, and death and how we can achieve our spiritual liberation by mastering the flow of time.

Now I understood why my father was wearing white. You see, in my culture, white is the color worn at the time of death. A dead body is divested of colored clothes and dressed in white. All those who are in mourning also clothe themselves in white.

The meditation started. My father told us to close our eyes, and we all sat, our eyes closed. We took a few deep breaths.

"Take your awareness to the time when your whole life will be behind you," my father said. "In front of you, there is a gate. Beyond that gate, what exists you do not know. And all you know is that you each will reach that gate. That gate is death.

"Take a deep breath and pass through that gate as you exhale. As you pass through the gate of death, feel your heartbeat, feel your body. You'll take a deep breath in, and you will exhale, and you will realize you cannot inhale anymore. Slowly your extremities will start to become numb. Your hands, your fingers, your feet, your toes. Slowly your heart rate will start to drop and then the heart will stop pumping the blood. The brain will be in a state of shock trying to understand what is happening. And as the oxygen in the blood starts to diminish, you will collapse on the ground, unable to speak, unable to understand. What would be the last thoughts before your death?" My father paused for a long beat.

"Take a deep breath, exhale, and go to the time when your body will be in front of you like a piece of cloth that you have discarded. And you'll observe your body that you cared for, that you had ego for. The hair, the eyes, the nose, the lips. How does the body look without any life? And even before you start to understand what is happening, the people who love you will come, trying to revive you. They will scream, they will cry, but eventually they will accept that you have passed.

"Take a deep breath, exhale, and take your awareness to the time when your loved ones have accepted that you are gone. They will accept your death even before you have a chance to accept your death. They'll still feel the pain, but they will have accepted. And in their grief, they will prepare your body. What is the final piece of clothing that will be put upon you?

"Take a deep breath, exhale, and look at the body being taken away by your loved ones. Nobody wants a body that has started to rot in their house. The body is being taken away to the cremation grounds. Take your awareness to the time when your body, dressed in white, is put on a pile of wood ready to be burned. This is the last time you will see this body. This is the last time this body will exist on this planet underneath the blue sky. Like everything else—the mango on the tree, the flower, the bee—even this body will one day run out of time.

"Take a deep breath and as you exhale, look at somebody putting the spark to the pile of wood. And watch your body burn." And as my father said this, I could hear the deep gasps from some of the older monks. I could hear them weeping.

Even my eyes had become wet. I did not have many possessions. But my thoughts again and again went to Babaji's dog Tufan. What will happen to him when my body is burning in the fire? For among all the monks in this monastery, it was only I who cared so much for Tufan. I provided his meals. I made sure he had a blanket during the cold desert nights. I gave him water to drink during the hot summer days. And then I would be burning. I wondered who would take care of Tufan, who would complete my chores.

As I visualized my body burning, my father said, "Take a deep breath, exhale till the fire dies out and there is nothing but embers. You are now dust. The body is gone. And then the embers die out, and even the people who love you will bid their farewells and leave. This is the last time you will see them."

And he said, "Meditate on the time when you have no family, no loved ones, no objective, no body, nothing to do. You are just dust under the sun. What happens now? What do you do?"

And as I thought about these things, it became very painful. What do I do now I'm dust? Now there is nothing—no hands with which to finish my chores, no feet with which to walk toward the temple or the meditation hall, no ears with which to listen to instruction.

What do I do when I'm dust? For the first time, there is nobody to tell me what to do; there is no goal to be achieved. What do any of us do when we are stripped of our work, our friends, our families, our possessions—all of the things that consume our days?

And it was at that time, as all the monks were thinking, my father said, "Take a deep breath, exhale, and slowly move your fingers, rub your palms, touch your hands to your face, and open your eyes."

I looked around me. His was the only face that was smiling. Everybody else's eyes were red. Everybody looked a little dazed, even stunned. There were a few old monks that did not show any emotion, for they knew exactly what they would be when they would be dust. All of us young ones: we had a lot of contemplation to do.

I took a deep breath; I exhaled. I bowed down to the guru and then walked out through the hall of the immortals, looking at their images, stepping on the stones placed by great monks long before me. Shrugging my shoulders to rid myself of the sense of death that still lay heavy upon me, I said to myself, "I think the mangoes must be ready."

I walked at a great speed to that tree in the corner of the monastery, thinking, "How many mangoes will I eat right now, how many will I save for later, and how many will I share?" Lost in thought,

From Destruction, a Seed Grows

I reached the base of the tree. I looked up and to my horror, I saw that every single piece of fruit had been destroyed. A tribe of langurs had found our tree. Langurs are huge Indian monkeys—huge to a ten-year-old boy, certainly—creamy white in color with black faces and long, long tails. They are bold, curious, and very fast. They say these monkeys are the legacy of a great war that was fought long ago, in the era of Hanuman the monkey god. Such legendary monkeys did not care that a young monk wanted to eat these mangoes. They had pulled all the ripe mangoes from the tree. Not even one they left behind, and around the tree as far as the eye could see were half-chewed mangoes and the seeds of the mangoes scattered everywhere.

I had been just a few hours too late. That was it: no mangoes this season. We young monks would have to wait for the next season to see if the tree revived enough to bear another crop.

The world is a balance between manifestation and destruction, the two forces that in the Hindu pantheon are represented by Shiva and Shakti. Great and powerful consequences come from devastation. In human history, the tradition of the Gurkhas shows us this. The Gurkhas are a very special elite military unit, one of the most decorated units in the world. They have served many nations—the British army, the Indian army, UN peacekeeping forces—and fought in war zones all around the world. The Gurkhas are known for their exceptional heroism in the face of insurmountable odds. In 2010, one Gurkha in Afghanistan singlehandedly held his post against more than thirty Taliban fighters. Another Gurkha, armed only with his *kukri* knife, defeated a band of forty robbers, *dacoits*, who boarded a train in India and tried to rape a young woman. Imagine it: forty ruthless thieves, armed to the teeth, whupped by a single Gurkha. They are simply the best of the best.

Now, one of the myths behind the Gurkhas is that the Hindu master yogi Gorakhnath was practicing the secret art of Sanjeevani—you remember, the nectar of immortality that Suzie and Barbara had pursued all the way to our monastery. The story goes that while he was practicing, a group of young children came to him. They were trying to make toy soldiers, and Gorakhnath said to them, "Don't worry, I'll make some toy soldiers for you." And while he was making the toy soldiers, he kept practicing the art of Sanjeevani, and the toy soldiers came to life. Because they were magical and made to be warriors, these soldiers were so strong, so powerful, that the guru did not know what to do with them. So, he went to the king of Nepal.

"Take this army," he said. "If you use them, you will have a long and prosperous reign."

The king of Nepal took Gorakhnath's gift and used these magical soldiers, who became known as Gurkhas after the master yogi who formed them. They served Nepal and protected the king and his people, so that this tiny Himalayan nation was even able to hold in check the might of the British invasion when they came to colonize Nepal and the surrounding nations.

This is just one of the legends of the Gurkhas' beginnings. People like to make stories a little more fantastical than the truth because then we can wash our hands of them. These stories are not real, we tell ourselves, so we need not take them too seriously. Gorakhnath creating magical toy soldiers is something we can applaud; it is a story that can make us happy. I do not deny the myth, but we who learned from Gorakhnath's spiritual lineage were told the story a little differently, in a way that gives it a new meaning.

From Destruction, a Seed Grows

Yes, children really did go to Gorkhnath when he was practicing his art of immortality. Yes, those children were trying to make toy soldiers. But it wasn't the toy soldiers that came to life. The first Gurkhas were the children themselves. And it wasn't that Gorakhnath put his art, his magic, into the toys. He gave that knowledge to the children. So enamored were they that the children went to meet with him every day. He would teach them the secret arts of breathwork, meditation, and asanas, together with the martial arts and the sciences of the Shiva Yogis. He trained them in such a marvelous manner that somehow even their genes started to change. They became the best, the perfect ones.

But then, in the midst of this good life, being trained by one of the greatest yogis ever to live, disaster came. In that part of the world there was invasion after invasion after invasion. It was a time of great hardship, and good people were suffering.

Seeing the destruction, Gorakhnath went to the king of Nepal. "Take these people," the master yogi told the ruler. "I have trained them, and they will give you strength to win your battles and help you achieve peace."

It is because of that sequence of events that the world knows about Gurkhas, and through them the name of Gorakhnath is remembered. If that destruction had not happened, that great yogi and his warriors would have disappeared from memory. Just like our mango tree and the tribe of monkeys: yes, the monkeys caused destruction, but they also spread the seeds far and wide. Unknowingly, they created a whole forest of mango trees. Baba Gorakhnath was deep in the jungle, tucked away from the world, training a bunch of kids and making them something special. But there had to be a disaster for the seeds to spread around the world.

As I walked away from the mango tree, back toward the center of the monastery, I felt sad. As if the skies mirrored my emotions, I could feel a few drops of rain starting to fall from the sky.

Rain is always welcome in the desert. But what I didn't know was that just like the antim yatra meditation that my father made us do that day, just like the mangoes' time had come to an end on the branches of their tree, this rain would cause the end of an era. This rain would be the antim yatra for our ashram.

The rain fell and fell and continued to fall. It did not stop raining. After three days, we started to hear news of flash floods all around the surrounding areas. People came to the monastery asking for help because their village had been swept away and the water was rising. As the water spread, we started to realize the toll that the destruction was wreaking on our lives. The cattle had gone out to graze, and they had not returned. Some of our people had not returned from the hills. As I started to look around at all the faces, trying to understand what was happening, I became very afraid.

The monastery was very ancient, and many of the buildings were made in the old style with mud and thatch. Eventually, the thatched roofs and mud walls gave way. First, there were twenty huts for a hundred people. Then there were ten huts for a hundred people. In the end, we took shelter from the rain in the meditation hall, our largest and sturdiest building. But as the rain continued to beat down, even the hall started to collapse. First, a flash flood took one wall, and I saw the paintings of the great monks being washed away. Finally, the stones on which the ancient names were written were swept away.

We moved to the Annapoorneshwari, the food hall. We ran, and

I realized there were fewer of us than in the meditation hall. And again, we took shelter.

I saw many of the animals float away. Each morning, I would get up after a restless night listening to the roaring thunder and the rain, and each time I would see fewer faces, and I did not know what happened to those people. Did they get rescued? Were they swept away? Did they jump in the water to try to swim to safety?

By now, I was exhausted: from fear, from running, from the misery of seeing my true friends, the animals, being carried away by the flood waters.

As the rain continued to pound down, the Annapoorneshwari hall that had stood for centuries started to crumble under the wrath of nature, until at last, no structure remained.

Finally, all that remained was a tiny island of land around the temple, with roaring water surrounding it. And on that island, I was with my father and his two dogs, Shanti and Tufan.

We were sitting on the edge of the island and slowly, parts of land started to give way and sink. I tried as hard as I could to hold on to the dogs, but Shanti wasn't as nimble as Tufan. I grabbed on to Tufan, and we jumped to safety. I called Shanti's name as loud as I could, but I saw the dog sitting peacefully on the sand as it collapsed in the water. And I remember staring at the water, waiting, hoping that Shanti would come to the surface, but he didn't.

With tears in my eyes, I looked at my father and I said, "Why is this happening? Why are you not angry, Babaji? Why are you not angry at Shiva? The monastery's gone. All that is left is water."

Babaji just pointed at the shivlings in the temple, saying, "All three are his forms: birth, maintenance, and death. All we must do is look at time doing its thing—spin. And remember, the circle doesn't stop spinning."

He told me to come sit and meditate with him. I was hungry, thirsty, exhausted, wet. I sat with my father. I closed my eyes, and I felt nature's fury everywhere. For the first time, the world around me seemed like a cruel place. In that moment, I could not meditate. I could not feel the infinity my father talked about. I felt extremely small, disconnected, isolated, weak. I experienced emotions that I had never felt before, and these emotions took root inside my subconscious. I wanted the fear to go away. I tried as hard as I could to meditate, jumping between every technique that I had learned—or could remember in my vulnerable state. Finally, I don't know if I slept or meditated or fainted, but I was awakened by a bright ray of sunshine falling on my eyelids.

It had stopped raining while I slept, and the waters had become calm. Just as fast as the waters had come, I could see them departing. As the water receded, I gazed at the mud extending around the temple. It looked as pristine as the mud on a riverbed, like an empty canvas, as if nothing had existed before. And I looked at the sand, which was still wet and glistening like diamonds as the sunlight fell on it, and I wondered where everything and everyone was.

Later that day, in the distance we saw lights approaching. It was a rescue party. People came, amazed to see that the temple was still standing—and inside the temple, a guru, a disciple, and a dog.

Our rescuers gave us water and food and told us it was time to go. As we started to leave with them, in the corner of the monastery I saw that not only the temple had endured: even the mango tree had survived. And underneath that ancient mango tree, where the monkeys had thrown the mango seeds down on the earth, new seedlings were sprouting.

Just for a moment, I felt like a mango being devoured by a

monkey. Seconds before, that fruit was ripening on the tree, beautiful and glistening. The next moment it was destroyed, crushed between the monkey's teeth, thrown to the ground, and buried. Is this how we go? I wondered. Or is there a seed deep down inside us that will sprout, so that life can persevere?

Thought after thought raged in my head. Before, I had done many death meditations, and I had tried to visualize every single scenario my guru had told me to, but my imaginations and visualizations had never before had such a profound emotional impact. I never could have thought this was what those meditations wanted me to experience: the feeling of loss and being shattered when your whole world is taken away from you. These were new feelings for me. This was the first time I had seen chaos up close. I could still physically feel the sensation of losing Shanti, and I held on to Tufan a little tighter. Every single noise around me felt like a threat. I felt that the nature I had loved, the world that had always given me good things, was now conspiring to take everything away from me.

The joy on my face was gone as I sank deeper and deeper into these chaotic thoughts that I could not shut down. It was as if a new mind was born in my head, but this mind was different from the monk's mind. This mind was heavy, anxious, chaotic—still in its infancy but extremely distracting.

Babaji saw me huddling close to my dog. Maybe my eyes gave my fear away, or maybe it was the trickle of tears that I could not hold back.

With great compassion, he put his hand on my head and told me, "You are stronger than you think. You are a child of the holy *siddhas*. Try to feel your power. Try to meditate on what you want. If you meditate on what you want, maybe the great Sanjeevani of the universe will listen and flow through you, and maybe you can manifest your own destiny."

My guru's words felt like a warm blanket on a cold night. They comforted me, and I started to think, *I have to do something so I never feel like this again.*

Maybe one day our lineage would indeed become extinct, but that day as I was being evacuated through the endless fields of mud and death, I said to myself, *The knowledge of my ancestors won't fade.* It was a brave thought, but then I asked myself, *How? How will it not fade?* The answer was clear: somebody must teach it. If you want plants to grow, you throw seeds on the ground, and if you want knowledge to grow, you teach it. That young me decided that I would be the one to spread this knowledge.

Hah! I was just a kid who barely knew how to speak English. But I felt that it was important to make sure that there are enough temples to keep this knowledge alive. When I say temples, I don't mean temples of stones, because I now knew very well that floods can wash such temples away. For me a temple was a living temple, a temple of blood and bone: people. Like Gorakhnath, I knew that I must teach people—to make sure the knowledge spreads and reaches everywhere, enduring beyond a single lifetime.

From destruction, a new cycle had started. Destruction of a fruit had allowed the seed to fall to the ground; destruction of the seed had allowed the plant to emerge from within. And I swear, as we were being taken away to safety, among the mango seedlings I thought I could see the Jyotirling glimmering. A new beginning had commenced.

But in this new beginning, holding Babaji's hand and with Tufan the dog lying in my lap, I felt like the dust of the funeral pyre.

And two questions lingered with me: *Who am I? And what do I do now?*

> ## SAMADHI
> ## MEDITATION PRACTICE
>
> Close your eyes and maintain a nonjudgmental awareness of your thoughts.
> Just observe and accept these thoughts and feelings as they arise.

PART TWO

MASTERING THE MIND
DWARKA

CHAPTER 6

TWO WOLVES, FIGHTING

गर्भ चित्तविकासोऽविशिष्ट्अविद्यास्वप्नः

The interior of the mind is deceived by the dream world.

Some of the saints in our monastery near the Aravalli mountains used to tell me that a baby cries when they are born because they remember the place of bliss where they dwelled with God before. Now they find themselves in this mortal body, feeling all the pain of birth, and they cry because they long to return to the divine place they came from.

I, too, felt like that child after birth, remembering the place where I used to live: the majestic monastery, the loving monks, the divine wisdom that flowed from every single corner, the sounds of the holy chants, the sense of mystic serenity in a place where time stood still. After the flood, I was snatched away, and as I went farther and farther from the monastery, I felt a deep sorrow taking root in my heart.

Until this point, in Rajasthan, I had only known purity. Now it was time for me to learn that there is duality within us all and a foe that must be defeated.

With my father and Tufan, I went to a suburb near Delhi called Dwarka. Because Delhi is so overpopulated, at that time the farmlands all around it were being developed as an extension to the city. In Dwarka, construction was happening everywhere, with brand-new buildings springing up in former fields. Dwarka itself had been constructed from eleven villages, including one called Bagdola. Planes roared overhead because the suburb lay just half a mile from the main runway of Indira Gandhi International Airport. Next to the village was a swamp that the people of Bagdola used as a place to throw their garbage—and as a toilet.

When we reached this place, I was appalled at the sight of the swamp, the smells, the sounds.

"We will make our new ashram here," Babaji announced.

I looked at him, so perplexed that I couldn't find words. Even Tufan tilted his head in bewilderment.

Finally, I asked, "How can we stay here? Are you saying we will be in the village next to the swamp? Or in those new buildings near the runway?"

"No. This land, here in the swamp, is where we will build our monastery."

Again, I was lost for words. Babaji smiled at me. "Son, it is from the swamp that a lotus grows, and it is on that lotus that Brahma sits." Brahma is the god who gives knowledge.

From this metaphor I gained a little peace, but I did not think it would last very long. Every few minutes a villager walked down to dump their garbage in the swamp, and just as frequently an airplane would land on the runway, rattling every cell in my body.

My father saw my discomfort. "Come, Ishan, let me tell you a story." He knew that I was always comforted by his stories, which would take me away from whatever reality troubled me into a wonderland painted by his beautiful words. Only rarely did he show me his softer side and any physical affection, but this seemed to be a special day: he called me near, sat me on his lap, and stroked my hair.

"Son, have you heard the story of the two wolves?"

I gazed up at his face, confused yet excited. Already this sounded like an excellent story!

"No, Babaji. Tell me about these wolves."

"There is a story—a fable, really—that says inside every person, there are two wolves that are always fighting. One is a good wolf, representing your positivity, peace, love, and divinity. The other is a bad wolf, representing your fears, anxieties, traumas, and pain. It is a constant battle."

"Well, but which wolf wins? No, don't tell me—I know! The good wolf wins." I grinned in satisfaction at my own cleverness.

"No," my father smiled at me gently. "Each of us decides which wolf within us wins."

"We get to decide? How does that work?"

"The wolf you feed the most will win," Babaji replied. "You feed it with your actions, you feed it with your emotions, and you feed it with your thoughts. Whichever is best fed will win, and that wolf will decide the fate of your life."

I knew this story was intended to be a puzzle for me to figure out, and I thought my father was telling me to be more positive. But that didn't make sense: "But Babaji, all my life I've been taught that there is goodness inside me and truth, and the only truth is goodness. So I understand the good wolf in me. But where did this bad wolf come from? If I am divine, how does this bad wolf come to be inside me?"

My father smiled more broadly, as if proud of my question. "Did I ever tell you about the *manas putras*?"

I shook my head. "No, Babaji, I do not know about the manas putras."

And so my father told me another story, one that showed me how the seeds of negativity can be sown.

Once, the story goes, the great Lord Shiva was sitting in peace, feeling utterly content. Thinking to surprise him, his wife snuck up behind him and put her hands over his eyes. Just for a fraction of a second, Lord Shiva was startled from his peace, and out of the emotion he felt in that instant, a demon was born. The demon's name was Andhakasura, and he was both blind and ugly.

"Lord, what is that?" Lord Shiva's wife exclaimed.

"That is my manas putra," he replied. "It is a child of my mind, created from my emotions. When you put your hands on my eyes, just for an instant, my peace was lost, and I felt something that was not positive. And from that moment of negativity, this manas putra was born."

In time, Andhakasura grew up, and he caused a lot of havoc. Eventually, Lord Shiva had to fight this manas putra, and only then was there peace once more.

All sorrows, my father explained to me, are the manas putras. We, too, are Lord Shiva, and each time we experience suffering, we create a baby negative emotion that will grow up to be a big, strong demon negative emotion. Eventually, we will have to fight it and defeat it so that peace returns to our lives.

You might think of it like the evil Lord Voldemort in the Harry Potter books. At first, Voldemort was weak, but then as he fed his power, he grew stronger. Eventually, he became the terrible foe that Harry had to defeat.

In the simplest terms, I could understand the connection with Babaji's wolf story. The sorrow and disturbance I was feeling now was like a little wolf, or a tiny demon. If I fed it, that wolf—that *manas putra*, child of my mind—would grow stronger and stronger. And if the bad wolf won, I would never reach my full potential. Bound by my fears, my anger, my disappointment, I would not allow the god within to come to the surface.

This is the great spiritual catastrophe we all must face—and overcome. It is what happens when the bad wolf, the child of our emotions, is fed: we become limited by negativity and live our lives in a state of illusion, not knowing the divinity that lies within reach.

Only once was Lord Shiva startled, and from that one reaction, the demon Andhakasura was born. In Dwarka, I found myself giving birth to a thousand Andhakasuras every day! So many negative emotions. After that first day, I realized that in between the runway and the swamp where the ashram was being built there was also a railway track. Every three minutes a plane would land, and every half an hour a train would go by, its whistle shrieking. This went on twenty-four hours a day, seven days a week. Every morning the people from the village would walk down to the swamp to relieve themselves, and every afternoon they would come to dump their garbage. In the evening we set about cooking food for the poor people in the village because it was our duty to feed them and care for them.

Compared to the serenity of Aravalli, it felt like chaos, and I felt there was no escape for me.

I started to wonder, *Why is there so much frenzy in the world? Where are all these planes coming from, and where are they going? And those trains: Where are all those people traveling to? How many of them are old? How many young? How many sick? How many will live a long life? How many will die in a month?*

When the villagers came to dump their garbage, I would ask myself, *What are they doing in their houses to create so much waste?* I felt aggrieved and resentful to be on the receiving end of it all.

In the evening it was my job to cook samosas and *laddu*—sweet balls made of flour, sugar, and ghee—and distribute them to the poor children. I would look at them and see the pain in their eyes, but sometimes I would also see how wily they were. "Brother," they would say to me, "I have a younger sister at home, can you give me two samosas and two laddu?" I had a limited amount of food, but looking at these kids, my heart would melt. I would give them two portions, knowing very well that there was no little sister at home with whom they would share their samosas and their laddus.

Afterward, I would go to my father and ask him, "Why is there such chaos and suffering in the world?"

This was at the time when the ashram was being constructed, so Babaji would use whatever materials he had at hand to teach me through metaphors. Here in Dwarka, my father did not look as angelic as he used to back in Alwar. There, he would drape a vast piece of cloth around him. I knew it was big because once it was my task to wash it. It was almost three meters long, and all of us young children had to work together to wash and clean and dry it. When we were done, Babaji draped that cloth around him, and he looked so beautiful. Sometimes when there was a breeze, a little bit of the cloth would flutter from his shoulders, like a cape. He would walk about, his eyes twinkling, with a majestic aura. But in Dwarka, we had very few people to help with the construction of the new ashram, so Babaji was down there in the mud, carrying building materials around, doing all that he could. Gone was that magnificent cloth flowing around him. Now he wore once-white overalls that were ragged and stained with great smears of dirt. Seeing him, you would never think he was a great guru from an ancient and revered lineage.

Now he led me over to one of the buildings being constructed and said, "Ishan, look at this." He showed me a window leaning against a wall, ready to be installed.

"Yes, that's a very nice window," I told him, not understanding why he was showing it to me.

Then my father picked up the window and hoisted it into a large hole in the wall, where he would fix it in place.

"What is this window made up of?" he asked me.

"Well, glass," I replied.

"Indeed. Now look through the window and tell me what you see."

"I see the sun. I see some birds—pigeons. I see the construction site. I see the village beyond."

"Excellent," he said. Then he picked up some black paste and applied it to one side of the window. Now the window started to look like a mirror.

"Now what do you see?" Babaji asked me.

"I see myself."

"That's right. And our minds are like that glass," he explained. "When we are pure, divine, in harmony with ourselves, our minds are like a window to the universe. We can see such beauty in nature and in divinity: we can observe, we can create, we can be poetic, we can experience the light.

"But the manas putra, the negative experience and emotion, is like black paint on the window. As the black paint becomes denser and denser, the only thing we can see is our own selves. Not only that, we do not see the best version of ourselves. And we get frustrated because those around us can see so much, but we see only ourselves."

He went on, "The saints are the ones whose glass is completely clean, like a big French window through which they can see everything glorious that there is to behold. Then there are some wise people who can peek into the universe and get glimpses of light through little holes and gaps in the black paint. And then there are so many people whose windows have become entirely mirrors, and they are stuck in certain situations, and they are very sad."

I looked at the window that had become a mirror, and I asked Babaji, "What can we do to make the mirror back into a window?"

"Clean it up," he answered, and tossed a rag into my hands.

It took me a long time to clean that window, rubbing the rag up and down, over and over again. Finally, after hours, the window was clean. I looked up at my father.

"Now I understand. We must clean our minds of the demons that we create, that limit us to our own small realities."

Babaji smiled. "Cleaning is hard work. Cleaning requires perseverance."

I could see now that we each must put in the work so that we can perceive another, more deeply spiritual, realm. In Dwarka, I would learn to do this through yogic breathwork techniques to rejuvenate the body and mind, samadhis to rewire the brain, and asanas to awaken my faculties. I came to understand that sometimes we ourselves paint the glass; other times trauma paints it, or society paints it. Meditation allows us to cleanse ourselves of our mental constructs.

Through meditation we clear the glass, so that we can hear music like Mozart, see beauty like Monet, taste food like a Michelin chef.

This was my first lesson of the immortals: learn to purify through discipline.

It was not long before our new ashram was constructed. We fell into the daily routine of rituals that I had learned in Rajasthan. By repeating the same day over and over again, we learned perseverance.

There were just a few elements that made up the protocol. Early in the morning, I had to go down to a hole that had been dug, and around it a *yagyashala* had been constructed: a worship hall where fire sacrifices, or *yagyas*, were made. Before anybody in the village had woken up—the only things stirring were the incessant planes landing—I would do a yagya, chanting an offering to the fire. This had to be done as part of the purification process. After the yagya, there followed *jup*: at least half an hour of chanting and repeating the mantra, again and again.

The second part of the protocol in Dwarka was *seva*, which translates as "service," but it means more than that. It means to serve selflessly, without the existence of one's own identity. I would spend a big portion of my day taking care of the villagers who came to dump garbage in the swamp around me. Unconditionally and without judgment, I had to help prepare food that we would distribute to the villagers.

Once the seva was done, the third ritual was *arti*, gratitude. Even though the planes were still roaring above us, the swamp was still reeking, the train was still screeching, and the villagers for whom I had worked so hard were still dumping their garbage in the swamp,

I would have to thank the divine and the universe. No matter how the day was, we forced ourselves to find something to be grateful for. Anything. Arti had to be done.

In Rajasthan, the daily repetition of activities was easy, beautiful; it flowed. It was like a natural process, in which a flower bursts open and releases the seeds inside to the wind. The seed lands on the ground, the rain falls, and the seed germinates, pushing up through the soil to produce a new shoot. No effort is involved; it is a natural flow.

In Dwarka, it was different. Every morning, people came to the swamp to toss their garbage and empty their bowels. Planes roared, trains thundered, children shouted, couples fought and screamed. This was not flow; this was chaos! Following the rituals in Dwarka was twenty thousand times harder than it had been in Rajasthan. I had already learned discipline, but here the lesson was not about doing the same thing over and over again. Here, the lesson was doing yagya, jup, seva, and arti irrespective of the chaos around me.

These four practices that formed the trunk and branches of my day are accessible, even vital, to us all: worship, whether through prayer or mantras or any other form; service without judgment; gratitude, no matter what the day holds; and contemplation of what we have learned in that day.

If you walk on the surface of the moon, the gravity is very weak so you will bounce along and even fly off the ground. But on Jupiter, gravity is much stronger, so you will be trudging along. A few steps will take all your strength. In Dwarka, it was the same: the simplest rituals were so much harder because of all the distractions weighing me down. I had already learned discipline to do the same thing over and over; now, I had to find the motivation to do these things irrespective of what was happening around me.

At the end of each day, the very last thing that came before sleep was meditation: the *sadhana* practice. This was a time to contemplate the things we had learned that day and then write in the Golden Book, answering a simple question: What do I want? Every single night, we were taught to answer this question. Of course, over time your answer would change. That did not matter. It was never about what the goal was; it was about simply having a goal.

Back when I was in Rajasthan, I never asked myself this question. I was happy and content. And even if someone had asked me this question—What do you want?—it would probably have taken me a long time to think of an answer.

Now in Dwarka, every day I wanted twenty things! For the planes to stop flying, for the train to stop running, for the garbage to stop being dumped. For me to get away from this swamp and go back to Rajasthan. I wanted so many things that every day I had much to write in the Golden Book. Yet as I wrote I would wonder, *Is it the Shiva in me that is writing this book, or the Andhakasura that is speaking for me?*

Many, many days passed like this. The days became months, and the months turned into years, until finally some things started to change. I realized that, through perseverance, the activities that created positivity had become much stronger than the activities that created negativity. The yagya became more powerful, the seva became more heartfelt, the arti created more joy. And through years and years of contemplation on that question, *What do I want?* a clearer image was starting to emerge.

When you excel at something, inevitably ego arises. I didn't know it then, but when you become good at spirituality, even a spiritual ego can grow. I started to feel a sense of superiority. I became proud, feeling that I was somehow better than other people because I was able to accomplish something that they could not. In my innocence, I was unknowingly feeding the bad wolf and giving strength to the manas putra through my unchecked thoughts and emotions.

This was one of the biggest lessons I had to learn from Dwarka, but it wasn't until I left that place that I truly understood it.

> **SAMADHI MEDITATION PRACTICE**
>
> Close your eyes, relax, and bring your awareness to a positive, divine, and happy memory. Relive and experience the feeling and energy of that moment, and meditate on that energy.

CHAPTER 7
FORGETTING OUR DIVINE NATURE

चित्तं मन्त्रः

Mantra stills the mind.

There came a time in Hanuman's life when he forgot that he was immortal: that he had been blessed with the wisdom of the ages, the strength of the universe, the power of the elements. He developed amnesia and so became limited by his mortal form. He started to live life like an ordinary man, forgetting his true potential.

The story goes that Hanuman, along with the army of Sugriva, was helping Lord Rama find his wife, Sita. She had been carried off by Ravana, ruler of the island kingdom of Lanka. In their search for Sita, they marched all the way to the southernmost point of India. They knew they had to get across to Lanka, but a vast ocean lay between. Everyone started to ponder and discuss, "How will we reach the island?"

Many of them became tense and filled with fear. Even the strongest warriors among them were thinking it was an impossible task—that no matter how hard they tried, they could get only a fraction of the way across the ocean. Hanuman—the most exceptional warrior of them all—was sitting among them, scratching his head and sharing their doubts and anxieties, for he had forgotten his own powers.

It is said that a lion cub adopted by dogs may start to live his life like his companions, forgetting the strength of his own species. So it was at that time as all assembled were pondering, debating, worrying, that the wise men of the legion decided it was time somebody reminded Hanuman who he truly was. For he was the one with the strength to fly to Lanka and rescue Sita. And he did: after a saint reminded him of his power, Hanuman took a mighty step across the ocean and found Sita. It was like his prati prasav, where knowledge was given to him—or rather, reinstalled in him. Hanuman rediscovered his inner divinity and soared across the ocean to fulfill his destiny.

Each one of us goes through the same amnesia that Hanuman suffered from. We forget our strength, we forget our divine nature, and then somebody has to remind us of who we are—remind us we are Hanuman.

In Dwarka, I started to get this same amnesia. Day by day, I was beginning to forget Rajasthan. You see, I was too busy surviving, and there were so many distractions to disorient me. Living in a city such as Delhi, it is as if the entire rain of the season falls on your head in one raindrop. Not just one time, but in each and every moment, a sensory monsoon dumps on you all at once. Sensations and distractions are everywhere. Humans are a little like sponges: we assimilate the energies that are around us. I would witness people who were angry, and somehow I would feel their anger too. Day by day, inch by inch, the sights, sounds, and smells around me saturated me.

I was disconnected from my past, from the wisdom and practices I had found in Rajasthan, and every day in this new life I was living, I would end up creating one manas putra or another. Frustration, anger, annoyance—bad wolves were abounding in my mind.

I puzzled and agonized over questions about suffering and chaos. Even though I myself was not living a glamorous existence, dwelling in a small ashram built on a swamp alongside a village that disposed of its garbage on my doorstep, there were always people who had far less than me. I would look at them and think, *Why does such pain exist in this beautiful land of the creator?*

The manas putra is also known as our dark passenger: it is the shadow self, the demons that live within each of us. Sometimes, though, this dark passenger slides into the driver's seat and takes over. When that happens, cosmic amnesia results because our divine self takes a back seat. It never dies because it is immortal, but it becomes weaker, and it starts to flicker. At the same time, the manas putra grows ever stronger.

When this amnesia overtakes a person, the biggest change that starts to happen in their mind is the thought *I am a victim of my circumstances, of destiny*. And truly, being a child in Dwarka, there was not a lot I could control. I could not control the sounds battering me, or the thoughts and questions saturating my mind, or the sensation that I was like a boat drifting away from the island, at the mercy of the ocean waves.

At that time, the saints took pity on me, just as they had with Hanuman when they sent a saint to remind him who he was. One day, when I was sitting in my room with Tufan, Babaji walked in. You could always sense him coming, even before he entered the room. It was like precognition: you could feel his presence, even before you heard his footsteps or saw his figure. That day the hair on the back of my neck stood up, and I looked to the doorway, ready to greet him.

As always, his face was calm, and he was smiling. Looking into his eyes was like gazing into the depths of the ocean: you had a sense of great treasures lying beneath the tranquil surface. Mostly, he conveyed his most significant messages through his expression. It was almost as if the spoken words were a noise distracting me from the true message that his eyes were communicating.

In my culture, we believe that there are more powerful ways of communicating than with words. According to the Vedas, there are four degrees of communication: *vaikhari, pashyanti, madhyama*, and *paravani*. Vaikhari is ordinary speech, the kind we use every day. Pashyanti and madhyama are nonverbal forms of communication: our internal dialogue and sensory responses. But beyond these three forms is the *paravani*: the inner vibration, the divine voice. The paravani is the word that cannot be communicated; it can only be received. It is said that if a person is walking on the spiritual path and they are confined to the vaikhari or the pashyanti or the madhyama, they will never truly learn. It is the art of the paravani that needs to be mastered.

This is a widely held truth. If we go to philosophy or theology, you will see it there. The Bible says in the beginning was the Word and the Word was with God and the Word was God. It is talking about vibration because—What is a word? What is a sound? Sound is a vibration. Similarly, they say the ancient Indian scriptures, the Vedas, were not written; they were heard. People were able to tap into their immortal selves, their atoms, their vibrations, and in their vibrations, they could hear the wisdom of the universe.

I'm sure you have felt it too. You may meet a person, and you want to talk to them without knowing why: a magnetism is pulling you toward them. There is energy, a kind of electricity. It is that art of understanding without words that Rajasthan had gifted me. It was a skill that was taught to every child, like riding a bike. And although in my amnesia I had forgotten a lot, I had not forgotten how to communicate with my father. My every cell prepared to receive what he was about to convey.

Babaji entered the room, and in his hand he held a book. He put that book in front of me.

In Dwarka, we had a very primitive electrical system, and if something broke down, people had to make their own repairs—there was no electrician to call. When someone accidentally stepped on a bare wire, they would get an electric shock, and we would exclaim, "Oh, he is *cheapuk gaya*." This phrase means that the person is stuck. Having experienced it myself, I can tell you that when you get an electric shock, your muscles contract and you can't move. It's as if you're held in place by Super Glue. To free yourself, someone has to push or jolt you; otherwise, you remain stuck to that electrical current.

When I picked up that book, I felt like I was cheapuk gaya—my fingers were glued to it, and I couldn't let go. It was as if there was a powerful force being transmitted through it.

When I finally opened the book, I discovered that it contained divine mantras. This book consisted of just three chapters, but each chapter was profound in its own way.

The first chapter was quite simple, really. It contained mantras that allowed you to invoke the infinite energies of the universe into your life. The second chapter revolved around gratitude; again, nothing very complicated. It contained mantras that were sounds designed to remind you of gratitude, which you would repeat over and over again. The third chapter was much more complex. It was the sadhana—a spiritual practice to attain a desired goal—and it contained three hundred mantras. The words of these mantras didn't even have any specific meaning; they were purely a set of sounds and vibrational frequencies. The order of these three chapters reflected the spiritual path we all must take: invoke and embrace the infinite, express gratitude, and then go beyond words to the divine voice, the paravani.

I understood the first two chapters quite well, and I began reading them over and over again. However, the third chapter remained elusive to me, as it seemed like a collection of meaningless gibberish. Three hundred mantras of pure nonsense: How was I supposed to approach that?

As I concentrated on the first chapter, I saw it had a certain beauty to it. It was a way of inviting Shiva's presence and blessings by chanting the names of the great siddhas. During invocation, I experienced the power of consciously choosing my direction. Life is so overwhelming and disorienting that we often accept whatever comes our way without question, assuming it must hold some importance or meaning.

I recalled a story about a revered monk who had a severe cat allergy. Whenever this monk delivered sermons, a cat would show up, making him sneeze and distracting him. So, he declared a law: before his sermon, his followers must find the cat and tie it to a tree.

"Which tree?" his followers asked him.

He simply pointed to the nearest tree, and the followers didn't question it. Why would they? The monk did not explain his reasoning. So, they dutifully tied the cat to the tree before each sermon.

Over time, all the young monks saw that the senior monks ran after the cat, caught it, and tied it to the tree before the head monk came. The young monks argued among themselves, quarreling over the significance of this process. They made up some stories to explain it, and gradually those stories became accepted without question. This went on for years, even after the original monk's passing, because the next monk believed in continuing the tradition. "If my great teacher tied the cat to the tree, I will also tie the cat to the tree," he reasoned. But even the cat eventually died. And the monk said, "I will not give a sermon until another cat is found and tied to the tree." Off the monks went to find another cat.

It is crazy how we attach significance to the mundane elements around us, building stories around them and making them our reality and truth, reinforcing them day by day. This cycle continues until something shocks us out of our everyday reality and awakens us to what is known in my culture as Supreme Reality: the infinite, eternal spirit, beyond the perception of the intellect. When we experience such an alarm, it jolts us from our dreams, landing a shock to our central nervous system, which pulls us out of our own heads.

For me, that awakening was brought about by the invocation, by chanting the names of the great siddhas. Each repetition connected me to their light, energy, deeds, power, and grace.

Until I concentrated on the second chapter, I had never realized gratitude was such a beautiful concept. Just as there is heads and tails, up and down, left and right, wet and dry, I realized there is either gratitude or complaint. Complaints are easy; our minds have a natural affinity for them. Our minds are like carrots: if you put them in a vegetable stew, in my opinion they are not very appetizing. But if you turn them into *halwa*—a beloved Indian dessert—they become the most delicious treat you have ever tasted. Similarly, if we program our minds to complain, they will gravitate toward a flavor that does not give us joy. However, when we focus on gratitude, our lives begin to change in a delightful way.

The way we choose to interpret incidents is crucial. Take the example of the Indian poet Kalidas who, after a fight with his wife, became one of the greatest poets in India. Everyone fights, but Kalidas added meaning and significance to his dispute, turning it into an inspiration for magnificent poetry. When we believe that good things will happen to us, even difficult situations make us reflect: Why did this fight happen to me? Or did it happen *for* me? We start to ponder, meditate; we connect with the paravani of the universe—the inner vibration, the divine voice—finding inspiration in the most unexpected places. This is what happened with Kalidas; his fight stirred him to become a poet, giving voice to his emotions. But if I complain, I pluck each incident from its roots, strip away its poetry, and render it meaningless and worthless.

I started practicing and propagating gratitude with everyone I met. When people came to me feeling sad, I would simply tell them that good things would happen to them, and I would teach them a simple mantra: "I thank the universe for the good things that will happen to me." I witnessed the magic of this modest practice, realizing that gratitude added meaning to any event. This simple thought transformed people's lives. Even the simplest folks around me began celebrating life. A person who worked as a driver would tell me, "Since you taught me this—you won't believe it—I'm getting more green traffic lights, and I'm so grateful to be able to reach my destination faster." Children would come to me and say, "Classes seem to be ending sooner since I started doing this, and I'm so thankful."

Through gratitude, it is as though our brains perceive the world around us in a completely different light.

Let me also emphasize the importance of repetition. I started to think of it as swimming: unless you put in effort with each stroke, over and over again, your body will sink. And with that notion, the difference between Rajasthan and Dwarka became apparent to me. Rajasthan was like the Dead Sea: a uniquely divine environment where you did not even need to make the effort to swim. In Rajasthan I was surrounded by such divine people that I floated effortlessly. Dwarka, however, represented the ocean that covers 73 percent of the world. In this world that is reality for most of us, we have to strive to stay afloat, otherwise we will sink. Rajasthan was the anomaly; Dwarka was the real ocean, in which we need to put effort into each stroke.

Every morning, my routine began with reading that book. No matter how much I grumbled about it, I made the effort to focus on invocation and gratitude. By the evening I'd find myself sinking, so I would return to the book, gaining a bit of buoyancy once more. I realized that by doing something repeatedly, it was starting to change me, altering my brain, body, and cells.

Like Hanuman, I was reminded of my powers: I already knew how to swim, and if I surrounded myself with the divine in every moment of the day, I could float effortlessly. My amnesia was broken.

The book of mantras had fed my spiritual self, like a special diet to increase my strength and vitality. Now well fed, the good wolf was triumphing over the bad wolf. The manas putra retreated from the driver's seat once more.

But one question chafed in my mind: What did the third chapter mean? It was the largest chapter, more than three times as long as the first two chapters. If the first two had such a profound impact upon me, what divine riches could the third chapter offer me?

Maybe it was time to seek guidance from my guru once again.

> **SAMADHI MEDITATION PRACTICE**
>
> Sit comfortably, relax your body, and focus on a memory of gratitude.
>
> Feel the positive thoughts and emotions of that memory.
>
> Gently embrace and accept its energy, allowing it to flow from the past into the present.

CHAPTER 8
LIGHT MY FIRE WITH YOUR CANDLE

गुरुरुपायः मातृकाचक्रसंबोधः

The guru is the means
For awakening the energy in the chakras.

In the meditation halls of Rajasthan, there were pictures of many saints. Out of all of them, one stood out. Every other saint was sitting under a tree with nothing around them and a beatific expression on their face. But Parshuram was surrounded by weapons, tools, and trinkets. He had his axe, his bow and arrow, and many other objects I did not understand. I remember asking Babaji one day, "Why does Parshuram have so many things, while all the other saints have nothing?"

"Parshuram had many tools because he went on so many adventures and quests," my father said. "The other saints did not go on adventures, so they did not need such things."

"Why did Parshuram go on so many adventures?" I asked.

"It was his calling. It was his destiny," Babaji replied.

It is the same with the spiritual path. A person who is sitting under a tree in the Himalayas will not need many tools. They have their breath, and they have their mind. That is enough. But a person who is going through the adventure of being in this world surrounded by chaos, they need tools—just as a knight who is going to battle will require his armor, horse, and sword. Like Parshuram, that person will need many things to finish their quest.

In the same way, a young monk living in an ashram set on a swamp in Dwarka needed his book of mantras. It was one of the most important tools he required to survive.

It is said that in the beginning, Shiva used a mystical instrument to create a rhythm. Out of this vibration, the entire cosmos came into existence. The heavens, the Earth, the planets, the stars—all sprang from this primordial pulse. One of the things that was created were the *bija* mantras in the third chapter of the book Babaji had given me. *Bija* means "seed," so bija mantras are the seeds of the universe. When we chant these mantras, we are sowing powerful seeds in our lives, each possessing the potential to create the infinite. These mantras assist in guiding our minds into a deep meditative state, bringing peace and tranquility amid life's chaos.

It is not always easy for us to find that serenity. Our scriptures tell a tale of *amrit*, the elixir of immortality. It is said that eons ago, the gods—by which I mean celestial beings, those you might call angels—discovered that amrit lay hidden deep within the ocean. The gods wanted to drink this nectar of immortality, so they decided that they needed to churn the ocean, a process called *amrit manthan*. They devised a plan to use a massive mountain as a churning rod, and they used Sheshnag, the hundred-headed serpent, as the churning rope. But the challenge was evident: when they attempted to churn the ocean, the mountain immediately sank. In this crucial moment, Narayana (one of the thousand names for Vishnu) assumed the form of a colossal turtle, swimming beneath the mountain in the ocean. His presence prevented the mountain from sinking, making the churning possible.

My father once explained to me that meditation is the same. When we close our eyes, our subconscious is like the vast ocean containing the elixir of immortality. In meditation, we attempt to use our conscious mind as the churning rod. However, every time we close our eyes, the conscious mind sinks into the depths of the subconscious. We close our eyes, inhale, exhale, focus on our breathing... and our thoughts start to drift. *When I finish my meditation, I will go grocery shopping. When I go to the store, I need to buy broccoli. I need to buy broccoli because I have gained a lot of weight. I need to lose weight because I have been invited to my cousin's wedding. My cousin has found love, and I haven't found love. I am almost thirty-five, and I haven't found love, and my cousin who is so young has already found her happily ever after... Oh my God, what is going to happen in my life? Argh! I'm so stressed! This is why I'm meditating. Wait, how much time has passed—one hour? Wow! Was I meditating all that time?*

This happens with so many people: you ask somebody to meditate, and immediately the mind sinks into the subconscious, and the mind becomes an enemy to tranquility.

The ancient siddhas from my monastery recognized that the churning process could become more manageable if it was done on the back of the great turtle: in this case, the celestial sounds, the bija mantras. When these mantras are recited, the mind starts to stabilize, allowing the churning process to begin and bring the amrit—the nectar of immortality—to the surface.

With the mantras, we can connect with the divine energy from which we all come and to which we return. This ultimate energy connects all matter, organic and inorganic; it is the creator and the destroyer. These mantras are the gateway to that supreme power. Our ego may make us ask, "Why do I need God, or even a guru, for this?" The story of the gods churning the ocean shows us how difficult the process is without the presence of divinity. The mantras help strengthen our faith and give us a sense of great connection with the divine.

However, there are several steps to this churning process. Subconscious blockages must surface before you will reach the nectar, and that would be true for my path over the coming years. For now, understand that when my guide, Babaji, witnessed me sinking in the chaos of the world, like a mountain sinking in the ocean, he handed me the divine book of mantras. This book served to stabilize me, provide me with a moral compass, and, most importantly, connect me to the celestial melodies—through seeds that would eventually, as I meditated, germinate into profound wisdom.

By this point, I had mastered invocation, connecting with the saints and their traits. Think of it like putting a location in your GPS in order to find a way. I had also begun practicing gratitude. However, the next step remained: the third chapter of the celestial sounds. I still needed to receive the *shaktipat*—the power.

They say that faith is the greatest gift. I have a vivid memory from my time in Dwarka when a team of scientists visited to conduct research on the effects of meditation. This team was comprised of physicians, endocrinologists, psychologists, and psychiatrists, all employing their various specializations to study the subject. My role was to be their errand boy—fetching tea, doing simple chores for them.

As I observed their operations, I struck up a conversation with one of the doctors, a Russian named Dr. Korotkov from St. Petersburg. (Needless to say, it was most exotic to me to be conversing with a doctor from such a faraway land.)

"What do you do?" I asked him.

He responded, "Child, I study the mind."

He explained that stress was one of the biggest factors affecting people in today's world, leading to burnout. Dr. Korotkov told me he would measure parameters like insomnia, anxiety, depression, and quality of life to assess how stressed or burned out a person was.

What struck me about Dr. Korotkov and his colleagues was that they were almost robotic in their demeanor. They seemed devoid of emotion, like a toy someone once gifted me in the ashram. You'd insert a battery, and the monkey would clang its cymbals, producing a monotonous clashing. There was no poetry or feeling; it was just a mechanical motion. Watching the doctors working, I could see there was much motion but very little emotion.

By that time in Dwarka, people had begun to hear that a great monk from Rajasthan, from the Shiv Yog heritage, now lived in the swamp. They would come from far away to learn from my father and practice meditation. Initially, these devotees appeared self-possessed and detached, but as the meditation progressed, they closed their eyes, falling into a state of divine bliss. Some had tears in their eyes, while others wore broad smiles.

Dr. Korotkov meticulously recorded his observations and found that, according to his data, anxiety levels were remarkably low among these people, despite the fact that they were professionals who had just come to learn meditation. They all experienced restful, baby-like sleep, enjoyed an excellent quality of life, and radiated happiness. One day, after making his notes, Dr. Korotkov closed his notebook and said something I remember as clearly as if it were today. "I don't understand what you people are doing, and I don't want to believe it, but looking at the data and the statistics, I am jealous of what you have."

Imagine that! The robot was envious. I pondered why this great doctor might feel jealous. Perhaps in his world, instant gratification was everywhere, but inner bliss and joy were rare commodities. Maybe in his world, joy arrived only after a sequence of achievements that takes many, many years. Study hard, study some more, then get a job. Get a promotion, then have a family. Next, have kids. Then study some more and become someone. Do this, do that, do the other thing, and only then will joy manifest. In my world, you needed only to sit, close your eyes, and—just like that! Profound joy emanates from within. The doctor was yearning for something that was already within him, if he could only prepare his mind to access it.

Dr. Korotkov's words lingered: "I am jealous of what you have." It made me wonder what was going through his mind as he walked out that door. To be honest, I was also experiencing a hint of spiritual envy. Although I was diligently practicing the mantras from the first two chapters of the book Babaji had given me, reciting the mantras of gratitude and invocation even though sometimes I felt no more than a parrot, I hadn't yet been able to venture into the third chapter: the celestial sounds, the mantras of surrender. Babaji had told me these mantras could be undertaken only once I received shaktipat— a connection to the divine power.

Think of shaktipat as akin to electricity. You can purchase the most expensive toaster, but without electricity, it's nothing more than an ornamental paperweight. You can buy the biggest book of mantras, the plushest yoga mat, but shaktipat will elude you because it can be imparted only through the lineage of gurus or directly from a divine being. There's a saying in my culture that translates as "Let your lamp light my lamp." Someone who has meditated, received the truth, and ignited the inner fire can spark a similar flame in others. This is shaktipat. In our tradition, shaktipat is an unbroken transmission, passing from one generation to the next. It is also a gift, given at the discretion of the guru, connecting you to the collective consciousness of all enlightened beings. It is an invitation to join in the power of their spiritual discipline. It is an access point to their great wisdom. Yet you need not be born in a monastery to receive it: any person can receive shaktipat from a guru. You, reading this book, can receive shaktipat in this moment.

I approached my father with great longing, telling him, "I am ready to receive shaktipat and learn the celestial sounds."

He shook his head, smiling a little. "To receive shaktipat, you have to surrender," he replied.

In life, surrender can sometimes come through grace to those born with it, like an innate genetic predisposition. Think of a musical prodigy surrendering to their art, or a mathematician surrendering to the Rubik's Cube, or a skilled fighter surrendering to their martial art. Without needing a great deal of formal instruction, surrender flows effortlessly. But what do you do if you're not born with this innate quality? If you're an average person navigating through life's tasks and responsibilities, surrender might not come naturally. The siddhas, however, have their methods. One avenue to surrender is through pain: a traumatic experience or loss that shatters the ego.

It was my good fortune I didn't arrive at surrender through pain. Instead, Babaji beckoned me along another path: service. He saw that the divine curiosity in me was starting to awaken, and my thoughts were becoming steady. He wanted me to learn qualities such as compassion, love, and selfless service.

One day, he called me and said, "Ishan, you live in this ashram, and it's time you took on some responsibilities within it."

"Babaji, what should I do?" I asked eagerly.

He led me outside, where a herd of cows awaited. "Your job," he explained, "will be to care for these cows. Feed them, bathe them, clean up their poop, groom them, milk them. After collecting their milk, boil it, and once the milk cools, skim the cream to make ghee. Use part of the milk to make paneer and halwa. Curdle another portion to produce butter, and use this butter to flavor the food we distribute to the needy in the village. Then put the ghee on the rotis we make in the kitchen for the hungry children, and distribute sweet treats to the underprivileged."

At the time, I was still very little. I had been helping prepare and distribute the food for the villagers already, but now it would be my responsibility, and the weight of it seemed immense. Yet surrender through selfless service and surrender through prayer, invocation, and gratitude would now be my daily routine.

My mornings commenced by rising early, tending to the cows, and, yes, dealing with their poop—there was an abundance of it! Yet I experienced an extraordinary sense of love in this service.

I couldn't converse with the cows, but I felt a silent communication with them, just as I had always enjoyed the greatest satsang with animals. I would gather their milk—an enormous task because we had many cows. Next, I'd take the milk across to the kitchen, where

I'd prepare the paneer and halwa. In the quiet hours before dawn, I'd sit beside the fire and engage in *yagya*: chanting mantras and offering ghee and rice into the flames to represent burning up the seeds of desires and karma. The yagya provided solace, especially considering Delhi's extreme weather. Delhi experiences a bone-chilling cold that pervades everything. In the United States, it's cold just when you step outside. The houses are heated, the cars are heated, the stores are heated: there is warmth everywhere. In the swamp next to the village, our only warmth came from layers of clothing. We dressed like the Inuit all through the winter! After bathing the cows with cold water, I took great comfort from sitting beside the fire in the early morning darkness. Its warmth enveloped me, and as I chanted the mantras and put offerings to the deities in the fire, I entered a meditative trance. During these daily rituals, it was as if in the offerings I would burn the manas putra—the negative thoughts that I created—leaving me feeling pure and innocent.

Consistency holds incredible power. Commitment, love, passion, and selfless service gradually transformed me, and every day there were little miracles. Each evening, I would distribute the food we had prepared to the children forming a long line along the swamp. There was a simple prayer I recited silently: "Just for today, let not the food run out before the line ends." For imagine the sorrow I would feel if my bucket was empty and a hungry child stood before me. How could I look into his eyes and say, "Brother, there is no more"? But as grace would have it, my bucket never emptied before every child was served.

One day, I was returning home with an empty bucket and a heart full of ecstatic, profound joy.

My father called me to the temple, saying, "Son, it is time."

SAMADHI MEDITATION PRACTICE

Sit comfortably, relax your body, and close your eyes.

Visualize a golden light at the top of your head. Imagine this light flowing down from your head to your heart and then to the soles of your feet. Now feel the light rising from your feet to your stomach, to your heart, and back to the top of your head.

Repeat this process three times.

CHAPTER 9
BECOMING SUPERHUMAN

मोहावरणात्सिद्धिः

Supernatural powers are a veil drawn by delusion.

Earlier, I described the way in which we are born. Before birth, we are one with God. Then we are removed from that wondrous place, and we awaken on this Earth, crying in our desolation.

A monk in Rajasthan once told me a different version of this story. "During the process of birth, the child is violently taken from the tranquility of the mother's womb and plunged into this world, which must seem to the baby a place of immense confusion and chaos. In the midst of this turmoil, the baby instinctively seeks solace in the mother's embrace, finding calmness once again. Thus, the child surrenders to the mother, resting in a state of peace."

Throughout life, the monk explained to me, as the distance between child and mother increases, many things change. What remains constant is our inclination to seek peace through surrender. We may surrender to relationships or to work, throwing ourselves into them utterly. We may surrender to entertainment, to gadgets—or to substances, trying to find peace at the bottom of a bottle. Yet, no matter where we surrender, the peace we once found in our mother's arms eludes us.

"It is our very nature to surrender. And in surrender we find peace," the monk told me. "A spiritual seeker is simply a person who is very cautious and watchful when choosing where to surrender. Such a seeker refuses to allow external influences to dictate their path; instead, they seek guidance from enlightened masters, from the divine, and from scriptures. There, they make their conscious surrender."

I have always held these words close, trying to remain alert about whether life is leading me toward unconscious or conscious surrender. Unconscious surrender may be a way of giving up, whereas conscious surrender embodies the way of the warrior. At that time in Dwarka, I was about to commence the next stage of my learning journey and experience what conscious surrender could be.

When my father finally ushered me into a room to teach me the third chapter of the book, he looked at me intently.

"Son," he said, "I want you to begin practicing these bija mantras and sounds."

He scrutinized my eyes closely, searching for any inclination on my part to question him. He knew that if I required him to provide me with a reason to engage with these mantras, I might not be ready. However, by this point in my life, through the practice of seva, through gratitude and invocation—all the things I had learned—I had undergone a change. I accepted Babaji's guidance as readily as a flower accepts light and rain from the heavens. In this acceptance, the flower begins to bloom.

The mantras that are practiced in the West often carry poetic elements, such as *namaste*, which translates to "I salute the divine inside you." In contrast, bija mantras lack glamor or poetry; they are just sounds to be repeated again and again and again.

Babaji and I sat together in a small room. In the center was a table, and on the table was a kind of mandala called a *yantra*, which is a sacred geometry representing Shiva and Shakti, male and female, the father and mother of the universe. Such yantras are used as aids in meditation, one of the most important tools for a monk in pursuing their spiritual path. My father had made this one by hand: it must have taken him days to carve it.

As a revered guru, my father would most often sit on a comfortable seat: a nice sofa that was like a throne, elevating him. Now he sat on the ground on my right side, both of us on our woolen meditation mats.

I started reciting the mantras from the book, thinking it was a literature exercise, because as I read, here and there Babaji would point out a problem in my pronunciation, and I would correct it. By now I was used to sitting in one place and reciting the mantras for long periods of time, so this all seemed perfectly normal to me.

As the mantras continued to pour from my lips, I felt something like an earthquake from the energies they generated. A vibration passed through my body: a tingling sensation, like when your foot falls asleep and suddenly the circulation comes back like a thousand needles through your foot. Now imagine that feeling not just in your foot but through your whole body. It comes in waves, so at first you think it is just a result of sitting for such a long time. But then it becomes a pulse, and you realize this is something you have never experienced before.

Your fingers holding the book start to shiver, as if they are extremely cold. But your job is to look at the book and read the mantras. Each time the guru corrects you, the flow breaks, so you don't want them to correct you again. Regardless of the shivering and the thousand needles pulsing through you, your focus remains on the book.

By now I was confused about what is going on, but I tried to push the confusion down and hold on to my focus. This became a Herculean task: every cell of my body was crying out for help and demanding, *What is happening?* I thought, *Maybe I can just lie down, because the pulse is so intense I don't know if I can stay upright.* But my guru was watching me, I had a task at hand, and I had already surrendered to that task. So I had to persevere.

As I continued to read the mantras, that pulse became a spasm in my muscles, an uncontrollable movement in my spinal cord. My upper body started to rotate like a conical pendulum, sometimes clockwise, sometimes anticlockwise. I continued to hold the book, but my muscles were spasming, my fingers were shaking, and my lips were trembling—and then there was another pulse. Suddenly, the sensations stopped, and everything was fine. I took a deep breath in sheer relief—and it all started again. The tremors, the shakes, the shivers, the rotation, but a thousand times more powerful than before. This time, the spasm was not just uncomfortable; it was a level of excruciating pain that I'd never felt before. I thought, *I am about to die.*

Just when the pain became most unbearable, I sensed that it was not just me trembling: everything in the room was shaking too, and the mandala on the table was collapsing upon itself. The mandala was shaking with so much intensity that what seemed two dimensional became three dimensional, like a pyramid—a pyramid surrounded with golden energy. It was as if a vortex had opened and broken through the roof of the room in which we sat.

At this moment, I decided I must stand up. *Surrender is all very well,* I thought, *but I won't allow myself to die. I won't surrender to my fate, like the gazelle surrenders to the lion. I will get up and run or call for help.* Just as I was about to lift my eyes from the book and stand up, my guru touched his thumb to my forehead. As he did so, it was like an electrical current flowing into me. Now the spasming was uncontrollable: my lips were unable to enunciate the mantras, yet I felt that my whole body was humming the sound. I wanted to stop, but I could not. My guru's thumb stayed pressed to me, yet my spinal cord was rotating like a conical pendulum. His hand was rotating with me, as if it had become a part of me, and I couldn't understand how he was able to move with me when he was still sitting on my right side.

From his thumb, I felt energy entering through my forehead. I physically felt it going to my brain, then from my brain to my spinal cord, and then pulsing to every single nerve in my body. In that moment I could feel every cell, every organ. Suddenly, there was a knife cutting into the base of my spine. I tightened every muscle of my body, and I felt as if I was not breathing and my heart had stopped beating. It was as if I were being gripped by Sheshanaga, the thousand-headed cobra.

Suddenly, my guru removed his thumb from my forehead, and I felt the knife pulled out. Just like that, I could breathe again, but now I felt the book sucking me in, just as light is sucked into a black hole. It was like nothing I had experienced before—even now I have no words to describe what was happening. It was as if I were a comet flying through the universe, but at the same time, I was moving through the book into the vortex of the mandala. Each time my spine rotated, I rotated through the universe and back (I am), then again through the universe and back (I am). In each rotation I saw a thousand worlds, a thousand lifetimes. I was not experiencing these lifetimes, just witnessing them. I kept on rotating, rotating, rotating, and then slowly everything started to calm down.

Even then, I could feel a huge amount of energy in my body. For the first time in my life, I could feel every cell in my body, every hair on my head, every drop of my blood, every strand of DNA. I was aware of it all. Every single breath I took, I was aware of it, and I could feel its energy. It seemed to me that each time I rotated around the universe, through the mandala, through the book, I became more powerful, more dense, as if I had the mass of a thousand suns.

The night continued. Then my awareness of self was shaken as I heard Tufan barking, calling me to my daily chores. I wanted to move, but I could not. There was too much vibration, too much awareness. I had the feeling that I was completely in control of everything my body was doing, as if I was deliberately making my autonomic nervous system function, my heart beat, and my lungs expand and contract. It seemed that if I moved, I might forget to make my heart beat, and the stars would fall from the heavens, and the laws of nature would collapse. So even though Tufan barked, I sat still.

By now, my feeling of discomfort had transformed into an immense feeling of joy. From feeling dense, I had started to feel extremely light. My muscles had stopped spasming, and they were the most relaxed they had ever been. It was the opposite end of the spectrum. The joy I was experiencing was not a subtle joy: I wanted to laugh like a child laughs, the kind of guffawing you are gripped by when you see somebody falling in a ditch and it seems so ridiculous. All of the world and its chaos just seemed absurd! Then I looked at myself, and I could see the energies within me and the absurdity of my transient nature, and I wanted to shout with laughter. But I was aware that my guru was still sitting on my right side, so I didn't laugh.

"Om Shanti," my guru said, as the cycle of the mantras ended—for perhaps the hundredth time, but I have no idea how many times we had chanted that night. He took the book from my hands. But I stayed sitting there, still grinning, trying to hold the laughter down.

Out of the corner of my eye, I saw my guru's stern gaze, and I was a little afraid that he might wallop me. But he just looked at me, and I remained seated. Tufan's barking became louder, and the cows started lowing, ready for me to bring them their food. But I just sat there. Maybe it was the joy or the shock of what I had experienced—or maybe my body was waiting obediently for the guru to urge me into movement.

Suddenly I heard my guru's voice. "Ishan—go, do your work."

As he said that, consciousness came back to me, and instead of feeling my body, I started to feel *through* my body. I became aware of my senses. My eyes opened as if I had awakened from the deepest sleep or even a coma. My fingers started to move, but still, I could feel so much energy flowing through me.

I bowed down and touched my guru's feet. As I did so, I felt like water. I wanted to melt and flow and remain in that instant. But outside I could hear Tufan barking, on and on, and I knew I had to get up. It was as if I was in a dreamland, but this sound of the damn dog was calling me back.

So I got up. And the moment I stood, I fell down. I felt embarrassed because there was a way we must be in front of the guru—disciplined, respectful—and I did not want to appear helpless and uncontrolled. I stood up again, and my legs were like jelly—I felt as if I had forgotten how to walk.

"Go," my father said again. "You are late."

I held on to the wall, and somehow made my way out the door, closing it behind me. I felt intoxicated. The whole world around me was spinning at great speed; I felt if I tilted my head to the left, I would fall to the left. If I tilted it to the right, I would fall to the right. Even if I tilted my head forward, I would fall down. I tried my level best to stand upright and walk without moving my neck at all. I look like George Clooney's Batman, wearing a rubber suit in which he could not move his neck. I took baby steps. At the same time, my muscles were very relaxed, and I felt like giggling.

As I went outside I saw Tufan, looking at me in confusion because I had a big grin across my face.

That morning, I did all my chores to the best of my ability, but it was extremely hard because I felt as if I did not have any control of my muscles and my motor neurons. Somehow, I managed. Afterward, I was sitting, feeling a little better than before, still happy, thinking about everything I saw, trying to remember the universes that I had traveled as elaborately as I could, like trying to remember the dream within a dream.

Babaji came to me and said, "Now, I want you to do these mantras consciously and seriously. I want you to make a commitment to do the mantras each day." Not only did he mean each day, but also at a specific time, in a specific place, practicing them in the most intentional manner possible. This is what we call *anusthan sankalp*.

"Of course, Babaji." I bowed my head.

In his eyes I saw compassion, as well as a touch of concern. "Son, the shaktipat that I have given you, the power that you have received, it is the grace of the Holy Siddhas. It is the rain that falls on the ground. If you do not hold on to the rain, the water will find its way through the cracks in the ground, and it will be lost to the land. If you want to hold on to the water, you must make an effort. You must build a dam, create a lake. This practice will help you hold on to the water, otherwise I am just pouring water into a leaking cup. So tell me, what you are going to do?"

I looked at him and replied earnestly, "Father, I will do the practice for twenty-one days. Every day in the morning, I will do the mantras, and every evening in the night, I will do the mantras."

Seeing the sincerity in my eyes, my father was happy. He knew that I would fulfill my commitment, not letting a drop of the energy that had been bestowed on me go to waste. Why would I? Never before had I felt such power, such joy.

As the days went by, I could feel my spiritual strength increasing. Each time I meditated, my mind would align, giving me an ever deeper and more powerful reflection of the world around me. When you put metal filings on a sheet of paper and place a magnet nearby, the filings align themselves into a distinct pattern. So too in Dwarka, I had had many thoughts I couldn't comprehend and so many confusions I couldn't fathom—there was no pattern. Now when I did the mantras each evening, suddenly everything made sense. I could see the pattern clearly; I could understand entirely. In the morning when I awoke and did the mantras, I felt the power of the shaktipat.

I would not become tired or burnt out, as I sometimes had before. It seemed as though the core that now lay within me protected me from exhaustion, failure, and ignorance. Each time I did the mantras, this core activated, and throughout the day, it felt like an inexhaustible, infinite source of power, potential, and energy. I felt superhuman.

The people around me started to notice something new in me. They started to praise me because I was the best in everything I did. I completed every chore the fastest; my insight into every book, every learning, every conversation was the most precise. People started to say that I was a divine prodigy. "If there is one other even comparable to Babaji, it is Ishan," they said.

I heard what they were saying, and I started to believe it. So much supernatural power had been given to me in these tools I now had in my grasp. Like the sword of Excalibur, giving King Arthur the ability to win any war, the shaktipat gave me the power to complete any task or challenge that came to me.

I started to suffer from the delusion that this power wasn't something that I had been given as a gift, but something I had earned. I was enjoying the power and the praise so much, but I did not understand that the power wasn't mine. The divine power was feeding the good wolf within me, but it was also feeding the bad wolf, with its thoughts of pride and arrogance. When you throw fertilizer onto a field, it does not discriminate. The crops grow, but so do the weeds.

All the same, it was good that I was receiving such strength and divinity, because there was another storm about to come in my life. And without this core of power, I do not think I would have been able to overcome it.

> # SAMADHI
> # MEDITATION PRACTICE
>
> Sit comfortably, relax your body, and close your eyes. Focus on your breath, gently inhaling and exhaling. Let your body relax and accept whatever sensations arise.
>
> Notice how your breath changes with awareness, and simply observe.

CHAPTER 10
THE BALLOON TIED TO YOUR TOE

अविद्यास्मिता राग द्वेषाभिनिवेशः क्लेषाः।

*Ignorance, egoism, attachment, hatred, and clinging
to bodily life are the five obstacles.*

There once was a man who was traveling on the outskirts of a thick jungle. As he passed the jungle, night drew near. Afraid of spending the night in the wilderness, he was relieved when he came upon a guesthouse. On entering, to his surprise, he saw that it consisted of a single dormitory, with a hundred people all sleeping in one big room. He stood there, perplexed.

A monk came across to the gentleman and asked, "Why do you look so troubled?"

The man replied, "I've never slept in a room with a hundred people. What will happen if I get lost in this crowd? When I wake up in the morning, how will I know which of these people is me?"

The monk smiled and said, "I have a solution for you. Here, take this balloon and tie it to your toe. In the morning, whoever has the balloon on their toe, that is you."

Happy now, the man tied the balloon to his toe and fell asleep. During the night, however, the naughty monk crept over to him, removed the balloon, and tied it on somebody else's toe.

In the morning the man got up, looked for the balloon, and started sobbing.

People came over and asked him, "Why are you crying?"

"One thing I know for sure, that guy over there with the balloon on his toe is me," he replied in anguish.

And then he started to wail even louder. "But if that guy is me, who am I?"

At the time, this story did not make much sense to me, but now I understand: we cling to the qualities, activities, and roles that we think define us. As the sutra at the start of this chapter says: "Ignorance, egoism, attachment, hatred, and clinging to bodily life are the five obstacles." If we do not know who we are, it causes *avidya*: ignorance or lack of knowledge of the self. This ignorance causes *asmita*, meaning egoism or a false sense of self. Egoism then creates *raga*, attachment to the people who complement our false sense of ego, and *dvesha*, hatred for those people who challenge our ego. Together, they lead to *abhinivesh*: clinging to bodily life because we fear death—by which I mean death of the ego.

Ego is the man with the balloon on his toe. Because we have not answered the question, *Who am I?* we cling on to the fallacy that the man with the balloon must be me. The balloons that we think indicate who we are include our achievements, our appearance, our profession, our family's status, our religion, our wealth. We cling to anything and everything that defines us.

But sooner or later, any balloon will burst.

My balloon was the shaktipat: the connection to the divine

energy of the universe with which I had been gifted. Now that I was connected to this energy, I could meditate longer. My spiritual experiences were phenomenal. I started to believe that these things were happening because of my own virtue, and in so believing I started to feed the manas putra that already lived within me.

You see, when I was in the monastery, I suffered from what I will call "ego of heritage." I knew how admired my father was. How could I not? He was the head monk, the one who was prepared by Swami Jagannath himself, the master of the ancient lineage of Shiv Yog. And everyone knew that I was the son of the master. It was evident in their behavior. I would be pushed during training, but not as much as the other children. I would be stretched during lessons, but not as much as the rest. Somewhere along the line I developed an ego, and it told me, "You are better than everybody else."

Ego is the greatest poison in the spiritual path. From the moment you start to think you're better, you are in great danger. Earlier in my life, my ego was just a notion that I was great because of who my father was. But after receiving the shaktipat, I started to hear from other people, "This boy is destined for greatness." Whatever art or skill was taught to me, I would excel in it. Where others tried to succeed, without fail my work bore fruit.

As people began to praise me, I developed an "us versus them" mentality in which I, along with the Holy Siddhas, had to deal with the incompetence, negativity, and misery of the rest of the world. The Holy Siddhas and I had to carry the weight of the world on our shoulders, and I was very blessed, for my back was strong and I could carry that weight. That was how it seemed to me.

Then one day a music teacher came to Dwarka. Keshav played the guitar and drums and was a master of Western and Bollywood music, and my father welcomed him. "Why don't you teach the children this Bollywood style of singing? Maybe they can use it to create some *bhajan* [devotional music] that will appeal to today's generation."

When the shaktipat flows through you, your brain perceives patterns differently; it recognizes them more clearly. So when Keshav started to teach us this new style of music, I picked up every note, every song, on the first try. Keshav came from the world of Bollywood, where there were performers and competition, rewards and jealousy, and he knew that I was the guru's son. So he kept on praising me, seeing where his advantage lay.

In the ashram was another boy who had joined when he was older than the rest of us. He had suffered many traumatic experiences; his wounds had not healed, yet he was passionate about learning. Alas, he had no talent for music. Keshav saw that he was the worst student, and he started to call him a Hindi name that literally means the relative of a sheep. The sheep's bleat is loud and crass, so this name is a great insult. When Keshav made fun of that other boy, I joined in too, and Keshav laughed. I saw the poor boy hang his head in shame as I insulted him. After that, I never saw him in the music class again. I did not know it, but my father was standing nearby and saw the whole episode.

My father saw that ego in me. He could have warned me, but it is like this: You see someone walking down a path, and they are about to fall in a hole. If you call out to warn them, that person will look at you with suspicion, thinking: *Why are they preventing me from moving forward? What are they trying to hide from me?* This person starts to think you are the selfish one, preventing them from being their best self. As my father would say, "Sometimes a person needs to fall in a hole and find their way out, so they can own their liberation." He saw the ego in me, and he knew I had to learn my lesson. Like an eagle that pushes his chick out of the nest, even though the chick will fall many times before it learns to fly, one day Babaji pushed me out.

For a long time, my mother had urged my father to send me to a Western-style school, and not long after this incident, Babaji agreed, perhaps thinking that this would be the boiling point that would help refine me in my spiritual journey. Or maybe he thought that being surrounded by so many children, I would become humble.

At the age of thirteen, when I was in eighth grade, I was sent to a Western-style school. At first, I was excited. I expected that everybody I met outside the monastery would be like Suzie and Barbara, the Sanjeevani hunters—curious and open—and I would be able to help them find the nectar of immortality. It did not take me long to realize that I was merely an oddity to the other children, and I didn't like that. I was still just a kid, and I hadn't gone through the full inner journey to become comfortable in my own skin. So, I learned to hide my real self. Like Pinocchio, I pretended to be a real boy, just like the others. They would talk about things like cars or supermodels or Teenage Mutant Ninja Turtles, and I would smile and nod, even though I had no idea what they were talking about.

The other students had stresses that I could not understand. Some of them came from broken houses, and they were depressed. When exams came, others would be anxious and overwhelmed. Many times I wanted to help them and share with them what I had learned in the monastery, but children can be cruel. A few times I was bullied because I was a curiosity, the odd one out. So I kept quiet.

Ego—its two parts—makes us edit ourselves. In raga, we change our behavior so we can get more praise from the people who appreciate us, and in dvesha, we change our behavior to reject those people who challenge us. I learned to hide everything I learned in the monastery because I realized that those were not the things that people were impressed with. Girls my age admired older boys who had cars or who drank and liked to party, and I was this sweet, naive boy who was all about meditation.

The teachers liked me because I was so eager to please, which was a breath of fresh air to them. But teenagers can sense difference, and they were not kind to me. However, the bullying stopped when I began participating in the school's extracurricular programs. Because of my training in the monastery, I had particular skills that the other students did not have. Not just in my own mind but in reality: skills such as singing, storytelling, and martial arts, which were part of our core curriculum in the monastery. At my new school I took up martial arts, which was entirely unfair: I had been practicing it all my life, for hours and hours each day, but for the other kids it was just another extracurricular activity. So, I excelled, and everyone started to appreciate me. I took up soccer and debating and storytelling, and I was good at it all.

Every day in the school I would be given a new balloon, a new identity to cling to. "Oh, this boy is a number-one debater"—a new balloon tied to my toe. "This boy is a good martial artist"—another balloon on the toe. "This boy is admired by the girls"—one more balloon. The more I associated with this false "I," the stronger the manas putra became, and the further I went from my true divine nature. It was as if the flow of shaktipat was supposed to take me to a divine destination, but the flow was so powerful that I completely bypassed that destination and instead reached this place of avidya, ego.

Rather than tamping down my ego as my father had hoped, my experience in the Western school had the opposite effect. In the monastery, there was a rule that you never show off what you have learned. Here, I could be the peacock in the room, parading my bright feathers to win praise. Getting attention for the first time was my kryptonite: attention from the girls I wanted to impress, attention from the other boys who seemed so worldly—this was the base biological fulfillment that a teenage boy wants.

Instant gratification and the approval of others can be the enemy of immortality.

It is one thing to be better than everybody, but it is another thing when you look down on everybody, and I did that. My ego grew and grew. All this fame and celebration played havoc on my mind. Truth to tell, I was becoming a bit obnoxious, and my priorities started to change. In the monastery, all satisfaction is delayed. You have to work hard and long for the payoff, so to speak—the divinity.

Seduced by the immediate gratification and attachment to this false self, every day I thought myself most successful because every day I had more balloons to grasp. Every day the sense of "us versus them" became stronger: in my head, it was the Holy Siddhas and me against the whole world. But if all my identity was avidya and avidya was the balloons, then my balloons were about to pop.

SAMADHI MEDITATION PRACTICE

Sit comfortably, relax your body, and close your eyes.

Meditate on the three aspects of your breath: inhalation, retention, and exhalation.

Allow your breath to be deep and powerful, maintaining a gentle pace, and let it guide you into a state of samadhi.

CHAPTER 11
DRINKING THE POISON OF EGO

पुरुष बली नहीं होत हैं, समय होत बलवान।
भीलन लूटी गोपिका, वहीं अर्जुन वहीं बाण।

*Man is not powerful, time is powerful.
Bandits kidnapped the women, in spite of Arjun being there
with his arrows.*

A group of young monks are chanting mantras as loudly as they can. There is a bet: Who can transmit their mantra the farthest? As they shout the mantras, their guru comes across and asks them, "What is all the noise about?"

"We are betting on who can send their mantra farther than anyone else," one of the students replies.

The guru laughs heartily and says, "Oh, you will have to beat Bhagwan Dakshinamurti—his mantras have traveled far."

"How far have his mantras traveled?" another student asks.

And the guru replies, "Twenty thousand years."

Whenever we sing a song or write a poem or chant a mantra,

how far does it travel? Does it travel in space? Or does it travel in time, like a lifeline offered to someone drowning in the chaos of life, enabling them to find their strength and make their way back to shore? The divine power in certain words can span centuries, even millennia, to offer us a lifeline even today.

I never really understood this concept until great misfortune happened to me. I did not know that in my time of need, I would have to draw on the strength of all the songs of the great masters ever sung. In Dwarka, I had learned to connect to the mantras and teachings, which are the songs of the masters, but there is a difference between knowing and acting. What if we have all the knowledge in the world, and we do not act upon it? What if our ego doesn't allow us to trust our own intuition and energy? What if our ego blinds us to the obvious truth?

In a remote village lived a man who was known to be a great devotee of Lord Shiva. One day, this village was surrounded by floodwaters. As the waters rose, the man looked up and prayed, "Lord Shiva, come and save me!"

His neighbors were relieved. "This great devotee has called on Lord Shiva, so of course he will come."

Lord Shiva did not come, but a boat approached and someone aboard it called out, "Let me save you!"

Many people jumped on the boat, but not the devotee. "Lord Shiva will come and save me."

Some of the villagers stayed with him, believing that this great devotee could not be wrong.

Then a helicopter flew above them and threw down a ladder. "Come, let us save you!" a voice called from the helicopter.

The remaining people climbed up the ladder and boarded the helicopter—but not the great devotee. "No, Lord Shiva will save me."

His neighbors thought, "Well, he has called, so Lord Shiva will come."

The water rose and rose, and the man kept crying out to Lord Shiva, but he did not come, and the man drowned. His soul went to Shiva, and the first question he asked Shiva was, "Why did you not come to save me?"

Lord Shiva looked at him, perplexed. "Who do you think sent the boat and the helicopter?"

Ego doesn't allow us to see what is obvious. In his book *The Gift of Fear*, Gavin de Becker wrote, "Your intuition exists, in part, to help you stay safe—to recognize when something isn't right and to guide you away from danger." But the avidya, the ego, has a trick up its sleeve: it speaks so loudly that it drowns out the inner voice of your intuition. And the unfortunate truth is that when we grow up, our intuition tells us to do something, but the people around us— the ones in authority—rebuke us and say, "No, forget about your inner voice. Listen to us."

Gradually, a child learns to ignore their inner voice. And thus, when the avidya starts speaking, urging us to move toward fulfillment of the false ego, then the conscious mind listens—because all its life, it has been taught to ignore the inner voice.

When I received the energy of the shaktipat, rather than flowing with it, I started to manipulate it, using it to fulfill my own needs. The more balloons I collected, the greater the false identity, the more I wanted to use that energy to fulfill my desires.

There are very few stories of people winning the lottery and going on to do great things. There are very few child actors who receive a sudden influx of fame and are able to digest that fame in a healthy manner. What happens when you get so much divine energy all at once? Rather than seeking to know the shaktipat, you seek to control it. It is at that time something powerful must happen. Before receiving the nectar of immortality, there is poison to be endured and absorbed.

I have told you about the gods acquiring amrit, the nectar of immortality, by churning the ocean. But before the amrit appears, first the greatest poison in the universe comes: the *halalhala vish*. Amrit is the liquid that can give life to everything. Halalhala vish is the exact opposite. It is like antilife: it will kill everything. So when the churning of the ocean was being done, the divine beings expected amrit to emerge. But before the amrit, the vish emerged. When that poison came, the whole universe and all living beings within it were overcome with terror. They did not know what to do, so they froze. In their immobility, all they could do was pray to Lord Shiva. Hearing their prayers, Lord Shiva appeared. He saw the halalhala vish, and he knew that if he swallowed this poison, even he would disintegrate. So, Lord Shiva drank the poison to save the whole universe. But he did not swallow it: he held the poison in his throat. That is why Shiva's throat is blue; in fact, one of his many names is Nilakanta, meaning "blue throat."

From this story we can learn three things. The first is that on our quest to find something good, first we must endure the poison. So it is with everything: if you want to be a doctor, to get to the reward of achieving your qualifications, first you must swallow the poison of sacrifice, study, hard work, perseverance. Until we swallow the vish, there is no amrit.

The second lesson is that when the vish comes into our life, we freeze. I myself experienced this when I was young. One day, I was walking through a wilderness area, far from anyone, and I saw something moving in the bush. Suddenly, a bear appeared on the path in front of me. As I looked at the bear and its long claws, I froze. My state of panic made me completely catatonic, and I forgot everything. I forgot the mantras. I forgot my martial arts. I forgot where I was. Come to think of it, maybe I even forgot my name! The only thing I remembered was my connection to the divinity, and I just prayed: *Save me.* Saying that prayer gave me a grain of strength: just enough so that I could push myself to move away from the bear and make my escape.

And that is the third lesson from the story: divine strength permits us to emerge from the peril, disconnect from all the other voices, and connect to the amrit. For me, that was done through prayer, and that is how it goes with halalhala vish: when all roads look closed, we fall back on a divinity that we connect to, a divinity that we know, a divinity from which we derive the strength that permits us to emerge from peril.

It was a normal day like any other when I experienced the vish from my own churning of the ocean. After attending the Western-style school for a few years, I had now returned to Dwarka. On this day, a martial arts group was performing in our neighborhood, and I used to practice with this very same martial arts group at my school. The coach of the troupe came to me.

"We have a performance today, and one of our martial artists can't make it. Could you help?"

There was a voice inside me, somewhere deep down, telling me, "No, you should have nothing to do with this." But my ego was louder, saying, "Do it." The avidya is always looking to feed its pride, so even though my inner voice kept telling me not to do it, I shut that voice down.

"Of course!" I told the coach, speaking out the words my ego was telling me to say. "Please just tell me what I need to do."

In this stunt, one of the martial artists would lie down in front of a contraption made of bricks, and a small vehicle would drive through the contraption and over the performer. The contraption was made in such a manner that—though the audience would not realize it—most of the vehicle's weight would be supported by the bricks so as to not harm the martial artist.

In India at that time there were no safety standards. We could do any such crazy stunts we liked. I looked at the contraption. I listened as the coach walked me through the stunt, and I said, "Yes, I think I can do it." I was thinking how good it would be when people clapped and cheered for me. Despite all I had learned and gained, there was still a desire for approval deep within me.

Soon the stunt was set up, and I was lying down, imagining the applause that I would soon receive. The vehicle entered the contraption, and I heard a crack. The contraption broke, and all the weight of the vehicle fell upon me.

I remember pain: the kind of pain that, even if you try to face it, breaks you. The kind of pain that feels like a flooding river. I felt that pain coming from a distance, growing, increasing, and then suddenly swelling into a great wave, and then I faded into darkness.

When I awoke, I was back in the ashram, and the students standing around my bed told me that I had been injured. As I listened and looked at all the concerned faces surrounding me, I tasted vish in my mouth. I wiggled my fingers, I turned my neck, I shrugged my shoulders—and then I realized I couldn't move my knees or my ankles. The vish was in my throat: not killing me but incapacitating me. I couldn't move my legs at all.

In Dwarka, we had no resources to go to a big hospital with MRI machines and CT scanners. We made do with whatever meager medical resources were available and whatever half-baked advice was offered. It was assumed that I got hurt very badly and that possibly I had broken some vertebrae in my back. If the sensation in my legs came back, the road to recovery would be very, very long, but through rigorous rehabilitation, it was thought that I might be able to regain mobility.

As I sat surrounded by chaos—the planes roaring, the trains screeching, the car horns blaring, and all the other noises of the village—I felt utter silence within me. I sat in my chair, unable to move, and I realized something had changed.

Babaji came to see me, and I gazed up at him in despair.

"I can't feel," I told him.

"Your legs?" his face was full of compassion.

"No! I don't feel the Shakti from the shaktipat anymore. I know this Shakti is the Sanjeevani with the power to heal me. Why can't I feel it when I need it the most? Before I could feel it in every cell of my body. Why can't I feel it now?"

A smile crossed Babaji's face. "You're more worried about the shaktipat than your legs?"

I couldn't think what to say, so I looked away, hiding the anger on my face. My father knew it was there, anyway.

"Son, I connected you with the divine energy of the universe. You were supposed to flow with it. You weren't supposed to lead it; you were supposed to let *it* lead *you*. You were supposed to follow until it took you to your real nature. Instead, you tried to control it, tried to make it do your bidding. And so the Shakti has once again gone to sleep."

"Father, how do I awaken it once again? How do I get back my power?" I pleaded with him.

"Why do you want your power back?"

"My friends, the martial art group, the teachers, the people in Dwarka, even the cows—everybody needs me! They depend on me. They expect the best from me. I beg you, please awaken the energy so I can heal myself."

Babaji looked at me and said, "Son, you have gone far away from the truth. What do you think—if the rooster doesn't cock-a-doodle-doo, the sun won't rise? The world will learn to live without you; your friends will move on. And Shakti is not a puppet that will dance to your tunes. Before you reawaken Shakti, before you can heal your body, you must go deep down and listen to the songs of the masters, the voice of your soul."

Still I was distraught. "Please, please give me the shaktipat again," I begged once more.

"Son, I have given to you what I could. What I have given is not lost, it is just hidden from you. Now you must find it. You must dive deep in the inner ocean and find your amrit. Once your body is healed and you are ready, the Shakti will reawaken."

At last, I felt a sense of calmness. Babaji had said, "Once you are healed." He was a Siddha, so if he had said it, it would happen. Now it was just a matter of time.

I meditated on his words, listened to my inner voice, went deep inside myself. And I found myself asking one question, as I saw my broken body sitting on the chair with a balloon tied to its toe. "If this is me, then who am I?"

I had spent a long time mastering the mind; now it was time to master the body.

But that would come later. First, it was time to listen to the songs.

> ## SAMADHI
> ## MEDITATION PRACTICE
>
> **Shiv Yog breathing:**
> Sit comfortably, relax your body, and bring your awareness to your breath.
>
> Consciously deepen your breath while keeping your mouth closed, making it continuous and audible to you.
>
> Eliminate any pauses between inhalation and exhalation.
>
> Meditate on the sound of your breath, maintaining a steady, comfortable pace.
>
> Let your breath guide you into samadhi.

PART THREE

MASTERING THE BODY
LUCKNOW

CHAPTER 12
SEEING PRANA IN ACTION

ते प्रतिप्रसवहेयाः सूक्ष्मः।

In subtle forms, energy blockages can be destroyed by resolving them back into their primal cause.

I was sitting on a bus winding its way from village to village. Through the speakers on the bus played "Jeevan Ke Safar Mein Rahi," a classic Bollywood song that reflects on the journey of life and its challenges. This song says that on the path of life, we meet great friends, only to lose them. You meet them so that when you are alone, you can remember them, remember your loss, and feel great sorrow.

That day, the song was entirely apt as memories and emotions flooded my heart. I thought of the Rajasthan I had grasped and lost, the Dwarka I had grasped and lost, the shaktipat I had grasped and lost.

Now my path was leading me to Lucknow, in Uttar Pradesh. My last memory before leaving Dwarka was of my mother saying to my father, "Why are you sending Ishan so far away? He's hurt. He needs help."

And my father replying, "The help that he needs he will get only once he goes on this path. I have a plan for him, and I want you to trust me."

That conversation led me to a new ashram my father was constructing in Lucknow, in the remote heart of India.

At that time, I had no idea why my father loved swamps. Looking back, I see that he loved them because he delighted in a bargain: he was almost certainly dirt poor, and swamp land could be purchased for peanuts. Like Dwarka, our land in Lucknow was a swamp, but this was a swamp of a different kind. In Dwarka, people would dump their garbage; in Lucknow, the local gangs would dump bodies.

Our attempts to reclaim this desolate land had been futile. Layering it with soil in a bid to level the swamp proved fruitless. Its marshy essence persisted; if you dug the smallest hole, it would fill with water. Even worse, the area teemed with snakes—constrictors, cobras, vipers—and encounters with these reptiles were a daily occurrence.

The soil quality, unfit for construction, dictated modest, low-rise structures. Our most prominent structure was a temple dedicated to Mahakaal, the infinite, the centerpiece of our humble enclave. Surrounding it was a thicket of verdant gardens and lush greenery, where the monks cultivated medicinal herbs necessary for Ayurvedic medicine. Around the temple of Mahakaal were circles of shivlings, each made of a precious gemstone, representing different aspects of Lord Shiva. Each shivling also represents a dimension: heaven, hell, and so forth. As we mastered each dimension in our practice, we had to move through each of those circles, eventually coming to the Mahakaal at the center.

Let me tell you a little more about Mahakaal, who is another aspect of Shiva. Unlike the fierce and formidable image often associated with Shiva, Mahakaal exudes tranquility, symbolizing the eternal essence of time itself. Depicted in art as a figure of serene contemplation, Mahakaal is revered as the custodian of the cosmic cycle of creation, preservation, and destruction. His meditative posture and peaceful expression suggest a profound understanding of the intricate dance of existence.

Near the entry gate stood a hostel with a few rooms where teachers and visitors could stay, as well as a therapy room. This building formed one corner of our square layout. At the bottom of the square, cows grazed contentedly in a shed, while on the right-side corner I found solace in a small hut assigned to me. There, I was tucked away behind a wall of vegetation, like a troll that lives in the forest and only occasionally shows its face.

When I arrived in Lucknow, the one emotion that prevailed in me was joy. Joy, because for the first time in my life, I had a bed. My own bed! That is something a child in the monastery never had because you slept where everybody else was sleeping. The very concept of a "bedroom" didn't exist. We children might sleep in one of the halls, and if one day it was occupied with a major event, we were shooed away, and had to find another place to put our mattress. And then that area became flooded, so we had to find another place to sleep. Before Lucknow, I never had my own bed to sleep in every single night. I never had a chair—even though I now had a wheelchair, at least it was a chair of my own! I had never had somebody give me food because we always had to get our own food. Each day, that was a game of speed: you did your work fast so you could race to where the food was being served. If you were late, you missed out on the most delicious food. The later you were, the more dismal the food was.

In my first days in Lucknow, I experienced a mixed bag of emotions. I was being treated as someone special, and I was confused by that. At the same time, I was happy because I had a bed, I had a chair. And I had some peace because I had spent so much time with the mantras and practices in Dwarka.

One of the emotions that I felt was guilt, a heavy burden that I carried in my heart. The guilt and shame of having so much power, and then doing what I did. In my head, I was replaying all the things that I could have done differently to avoid being in my predicament. As I looked back, all my mistakes seemed magnified. I could see everything very clearly in the rearview mirror that I was blinded to at the time.

The only comfort I had was the teachings that I had received in Dwarka. Wherever I felt the burden of guilt and shame become too great, I would fall back on the mantras, the committed practice of the anusthan, and it would bring me peace.

Yet the thought *How could I have been so brash?* kept echoing inside me. My heart and mind felt numb, exactly like my body: I couldn't feel half my body, and I couldn't feel the Shakti of the shaktipat that I had felt before. All I had were my mantras. But such an unfolding of events was, I believe, a very divine plan to establish stability in my life.

Once, a monk told me a story from his own teenage years to show me how he moved beyond a sense of paralysis and found his divinity in the driver's seat of a Ford truck. At this time in his life, he had to learn certain scriptures that were supremely boring. They were so tedious that the young monk would run away. At four o'clock in the morning when it was time for his lesson to start, he would make his escape to a very divine place in the ashram that no one was allowed to enter. He would make himself comfortable there and go back to sleep. Nobody could chase the young monk, even if they had known where he was, because they would be afraid of getting caught in that divine place.

The head monk came to hear of his behavior, and one day, he called the young monk over and said to him, "Now that you're growing up, what is one thing you would like to experience?"

"I've never had a car, and I don't know how to drive," he replied. "I want to experience driving a car because I think it would be a lot of fun."

"What sort of car would you want?"

The young monk named a Ford truck that was popular in India because it was sturdy and reliable.

"OK, I'll buy one of those trucks," his guru said. Then he added, "On one condition—you have to drive me around."

"Sure, why not?" the young monk agreed. *What did it matter?* he thought, as long as he got to experience driving a car.

The head monk bought the truck, and his student was delighted. "I promised you I would drive you. Where do you want to go?"

His guru named a place that was the equivalent of somebody saying, "I want to go from New York to California." The head monk literally wanted his student to drive him from one corner of India to another.

Again, the young monk shrugged. So long as he got to drive, he didn't really care.

They started driving, and the guru started talking about the scripture. The young monk realized, "Oh no! This was his plan all along!" Now he couldn't run away: he was stuck in that car, and he had to listen to that boring, boring scripture.

After a few thousand miles, the student was desperate for his guru to finish, but this particular scripture is very important to learn. Every monk has their story about how they mastered this scripture.

"Oh, I mastered it under that bodhi tree," one will say fondly.

Another will reminisce, "I mastered that scripture on a great mountain, next to a mighty waterfall."

Later, when anybody asked the young monk, "Where did you master that scripture?" he had to tell them, "I mastered it in a Ford truck, on National Highway 44, just outside Hyderabad."

There is a divine simplicity in being stuck somewhere. Just as the young monk was stuck in that car, in Lucknow I was stuck in my body. There was nowhere to go. Yes, when I was in Dwarka, I was set on mastering the mind. But mentally, I was jumping from one place to another place.

Now I knew I had to adjust to everything that was happening to me, and the very first adjustment I made was accepting the thought *OK, I'm stuck here. There are some good things; there are some bad things. Good things are I get my own bed. I get a few belongings, and I get fed. Bad things are I'm not bringing value to anybody else's life. I'm not doing the good work that I was doing.* Without this service, this seva that had been part of my daily protocol, I felt adrift.

Empty minds attract demons, and because I did not have much to do, I would just think of the past and relive my trauma, and each time the pain and the blockage would become stronger.

The one place I found peace was sitting in front of Mahakaal

Seeing Prana in Action

in all his tranquility. Alongside Mahakaal was Mahakali, the divine mother. Mahakali, the feminine energy, is the driving force that actualizes Mahakaal's potential. Together, they symbolize the balance necessary for the universe's continual renewal. Mahakali is also associated with destructive force: uncontrolled infinite power, the raw forces of nature like volcanoes, tornadoes, and tsunamis. Her visage is fierce: her skin is black, her four arms bear weapons and the head of a demon. When I looked at Mahakali, however, I did not feel fear. I just saw her as the mother.

One day when I was sitting there, I felt my father approaching from behind me. He put his hand on my shoulder, and he said, "Shiv, Shivanand, Shiv Yogi." *Shiv* means the great infinite power; *Shivanand* means the guru; and *Shiv Yogi* means the disciple. This phrase represents the trust a student must have in his teacher that he is walking on the right path; a trust that can easily get shaken when life becomes tough. A student who truly trusts his guru would reply with the same words.

I was in great inner turmoil, so when my father said, "Shiv, Shivanand, Shiv Yogi," I was thinking, *What will I say?*

I looked at him and replied, "Shiv, Shivanand, Shiv Yogi."

And he said, "You trust me?"

I looked down at my legs, then back at Babaji and smiled a little. "What choice do I have?"

Babaji sat down in front of me, and he said, "Son, you have been a good student since shaktipat, but now let me tell you about the *prana* Shakti: the Shakti that must flow."

Prana is the life-force energy that animates all living beings. It pulses through our bodies along a network of channels that are neither wholly physical nor entirely spiritual. It's the energy that keeps us alive, and when it stops flowing within us, we die. Prana Shakti is the general life-force energy found in plants, animals, people. Sanjeevani is also energy: it is the highest level of life force, the divine life force.

My father pointed to an image of Mabhadrakali, a different manifestation of Shakti, in which she was standing on her husband Shiva. "What do you see in this image?"

"I see Mabhadrakali and beneath her feet is Lord Shiva…poor guy."

My father explained, "Here, Shiva represents the mind, and Mabhadrakali represents the emotions. This image shows that when emotion becomes destructive, then the mind is a slave to that emotion. It is powerless, like Shiva here, and emotion has taken over."

He gestured to another image nearby of Ma Lalita Tripura Sundari, yet another manifestation of Shakti, representing the beautiful and blissful aspect of the divine feminine. She, too, had Shiva beneath her feet. "This image shows that even in the face of positive emotion, Shiva—the mind—is powerless."

"Wherever your prana flows, that is what will manifest," Babaji explained. "If the prana flow is toward destructive emotion like Mabhadrakali, then you create destruction, whether you know it or not. And if the flow is toward Ma Lalita, then it is constructive emotion. The prana must flow, and you must master it."

I thought I grasped his meaning: there is a flow in our divine energy, and we choose whether the flow leads us to the negative or the positive. So I nodded. My father looked at me closely, assessing whether I was absorbing his words and ready for more. And then he continued.

"Every Indian scripture tells us about *asuras*. Do you know about them?"

I nodded. "Andhakasura was an asura, and so was Ravana. In English, we would say a demon."

"Asuras are just people who could not master the flow of prana," Babaji countered. "In fact, asuras are the most hardworking, the most meditative of beings, and through their hard work, they please God and achieve power. But the asuras let negative emotion control the flow of prana, so the energy becomes a destructive force. Rather than being enlightened by it, the power corrupts and consumes them."

This was a new perspective, but it made sense to me, so I nodded. My father went on, "Son, you too received a lot of power through your hard work. And you too let the negative emotion control that power and create destructive energy. But now you are ready to learn the lesson and make the Shakti, the energy, flow from the base of your spine all the way to the top of the head. In doing so, you will master the cycle of Mahakaal, the infinite."

As I listened, I could see the mistakes I had made, and I could see that I had had the connection with Shakti's energy, but my consciousness was not rising up—instead, my lower consciousness had directed the power toward my baser tendencies. Now I had a glimmer of hope that I might correct my errors.

"Are you ready to master the flow of prana and master the body?" my father asked me.

"Master half the body?" I said a little sharply, glancing down at my legs.

"No—when you master prana, you will master your body," he replied. "To master the flow of energy, your consciousness must rise. If your consciousness is stuck in negative emotions, then that is where the energy will flow. But if your consciousness starts to rise, it moves up through your spinal cord. The consciousness, the Shakti, becomes one with the Shiva in the crown of your head. When that happens, you will have mastered the Shakti."

He paused to let me take this in, then continued. "Just as I was able to give you the Shakti as shaktipat, you will feel the Shakti flowing through you."

"Babaji, how can I master the flow of prana?" I asked him.

"First, you must know yourself as deeply as you can," my father replied. "To know yourself, your skills of awareness and mindfulness must become stronger. You must learn to be in the present moment, free from the past and the future."

Then he chuckled. "Really, it's good that you're stuck sitting in a chair—you've got nothing better to do than be in the present moment."

Soon, my father would be leaving, and I would stay here, trying to be in the present moment. Before he left, he gave me more guidance. "In this next phase of your journey, you must do a deeper exploration of prati prasav, and you must help other people with it."

I looked at him, confused. "I am not able to help myself, yet you want me to help others with prati prasav?"

Once again, my father said to me, "Shiv, Shivanand, Shiv Yogi." *Trust me.*

"Shiv, Shivanand, Shiv Yogi," I replied.

Thus began for me a new and deeper exploration of prati prasav. You may like to think of prati prasav as an ancient form of cognitive therapy, revealing the flow of prana as people's emotions shift and energy patterns change. Once again, I was going deep into the practices of breath control techniques (prana), meditation, and yoga postures (asanas).

My father arranged for a teacher to come and guide me in these exercises. The crazy thing was that this teacher did not speak any of the languages that I knew. I was forced to listen to him with my eyes, my nose, my touch, observing things in a completely new way. This was the *paravani*: the divine voice, the word that can only be received.

My teacher helped me mature in a manner that perhaps I could not have if I had been learning from my father. Babaji wanted me to open my heart, to raise my consciousness, to overcome the blockages of guilt and shame that I had created. When I was with Babaji, sometimes I would be too proud to admit that there was any blockage within me—but with this new teacher, things were different. I could open up to him because a part of me thought that if he doesn't understand my language, then this is a safe place to let go.

When you give the prati prasav therapy, it's not a conversation. You're not exchanging ideas and feelings: the other person is dumping their thoughts and emotions, and you are just giving it direction without participating. You're forced to observe, and I think the reason my father made me provide that therapy was so I could start to perceive the flow of prana.

When people first came to me, I would observe how rigid they were, how emotionally constipated. I would assess their face and expressions, how their eyes would say one thing and yet their lips would say another. As the therapy progressed, suddenly, something would change. Their emotions shifted; they became more fluid. A vibration would be going through them. Sometimes it was so powerful that it was visible: you could see how the energy was moving by the goosebumps springing up on their skin, their eyes widening, their breath becoming deeper.

Now through the prati prasav, I could see prana in action, how energy flows in the body. Now I wasn't just speaking the mantras; I was connecting to the energy of the universe. Yet when I was with my teacher, it was hard. The first few days, weeks, even months, he was frustrated because he wanted to say what he needed to say, and I was frustrated because I wanted to say what I wanted to say. And neither of us was willing to listen.

One time I got so exasperated that I called my father. "This is not working. I'm not learning jack from this guy! Why can't we find a Shiv Yog monk who speaks a language I can understand?"

"No, this is the only one—you have to learn from him."

"I can't talk to him!" I replied in frustration.

He huffed a breath and said, "Son, you're not supposed to talk. You're supposed to listen!"

And then he said something very beautiful. He said a phrase in Sanskrit that literally means, "One spoke, the other heard, and that is how they both became enlightened."

So, slowly, I started to learn how to access the flow of prana. I remember the day that I finally felt the energy flowing inside me.

We were doing pranayama, a breathwork practice, and I was trying to listen to the sound of my teacher's breath. Because I couldn't understand his instructions, I would just imitate what he was doing. When he breathed fast, I breathed fast; when he breathed slow, I breathed slow. Now my teacher pointed to the sun. He inhaled deeply, then exhaled just as deeply, repeating the sequence a few times, which I took as meaning, "Take in everything; let the soul enter the body." And then, "Put out everything; let the soul leave the body." Go into the light, come down from the light. Over and over again, I was doing this practice. And suddenly, I felt that I wasn't in my body anymore. It was as if I was no longer even in this realm.

I gently opened my eyes, and I looked around. I could see beings of light all around me, I could see energy in everything. It's hard to explain, but imagine there's life inside each living being, yet all we can see is the meat packet around it. Now imagine if suddenly there were no meat packets—no packaging. All you can see is life itself: in the trees, the birds, the cows. You can see energy trees, energy birds, energy cows, energy everything. I was still in Lucknow ashram, but it was not the Lucknow I knew. It was like some parallel alien Lucknow where I could see only energy: life itself.

When I looked down at myself, I saw energy. I was healthy and strong; my legs were not injured. I could see the power flowing through me. And then I thought to myself: "If I'm energy, then I'm not bound by gravity. I feel like I can fly." The moment I thought it, I was flying, soaring above the rooftops and looking down at the world below me.

And then I thought to myself, "I am energy, so I am not bound by space," and suddenly I expanded. It was as if I was everywhere, all at once.

In a rush of revelation, I realized that all barriers are mental. I was thinking I could walk, and I was walking; I was thinking I could fly, and I was flying. The flow of prana from my spinal cord through the top of my head made me rise up in flight in that moment.

This was the power of prana that I was experiencing, a divine energy that is accessible to us all through breathwork, the mantras, and meditation.

I was enjoying this so much: it was like a video game I was playing in my head. And then I remembered, "Oh, my teacher wanted me to go to the sun and come back." So I went to the sun, I felt the light, and then I returned to my body. I didn't just come back gently—I plummeted back into my body, like I had dropped from the sky. In a great whoosh, I exhaled, and I fell out of my chair.

My teacher was still sitting with his eyes closed, doing the breathwork exercise. Now I was worried. "Oh my God, what have I done? I haven't been following his instructions. He'll think I'm being disobedient." As it happened, this teacher was a great master of Kalari, an ancient Indian martial art. He was the only teacher I was afraid of because he could whup my ass if I didn't obey him.

So I quietly got up and sat on my chair and started doing my breathwork exercise again. Suddenly I realized: "What! I got up and got back on my chair!"

I was wriggling my toes, I was bouncing my knees up and down, I was twitching with restless leg syndrome—and I was ecstatic. I was just waiting for my teacher to open his eyes so I could tell him, "Yes, we did it! This is done! Level two complete!"

Then my teacher opened his eyes, and he looked at me as I sat there, grinning like a fool.

"Look at my legs! I can move them!" I started jabbering in my excitement.

My teacher always carried with him a wooden stick carved with a spiral pattern. Now, he took up that stick and hit me over the head. Whack!

I blinked and shook my head. Message received. *OK, back to work*, I thought.

And as I closed my eyes, I realized that this wasn't the last day of the teaching. This was the first. It was never about the ability to walk again: it was about mastering the flow of prana. Maybe now, Babaji was saying, I *knew* it. But now I had to *master* it.

SAMADHI MEDITATION PRACTICE

Sit comfortably, relax your body, and close your eyes. Begin Shiv Yog breathing at a moderate pace. Consciously deepen your breath while keeping your mouth closed, making it continuous and audible to you.

Eliminate any pauses between inhalation and exhalation.

As you breathe, observe your emotions as they arise. Breathe into each emotion and witness whatever unfolds, all at a comfortable pace.

CHAPTER 13
TAKING THE FIRST STEPS TO IMMORTALITY

शक्तिचक्रसंधाने विश्वसंहारः।

On uniting the energy in the chakras,
The universe ceases to exist.

I sat in my room, gazing out the window at the birds chirping in a nearby tree. As the little birds chirped and fluttered about, I was daydreaming about the day I received the shaktipat and the remarkable experience of traveling around the universe. In daydreams, we relive our deepest desires. As a monk, I had never experienced much desire, but now every chance I got, my mind transported me back to the shaktipat.

Suddenly, the birds flew away, replaced by a crow. "Caw!" it screeched, as if Kakbhushundi himself, cursed to be a crow, were awakening me from my daydream. I looked down and saw before me a pile of scriptures on the topic of prati prasav. The task my father had given me—to help guide people into prati prasav—looked impossible. In Dwarka, I was responsible for cleaning up the cow manure, which was such an easy task. You find the manure, you shovel it up, and you throw it on the dung heap. Job done. There is always a simple math to it: a cow can generate only so much poop. Now, with the prati prasav, I was responsible for cleaning out people's emotional garbage, and there is no math in that. A fifteen-year-old might carry more trauma within their self than a seventy-five-year-old. I could work on somebody for days getting rid of their emotional garbage, but the next time they came back, it was as if I had not done anything at all, and we were back at the point from where we started.

I knew that the root cause of their relapses was avidya: the lack of awareness of who they truly were. No matter how many skills I taught those people, how much time I spent with them, something innately human in them made them nod approvingly when they were with me but forget it all each time they went back to their lives. From vidya—knowledge of self—they returned to avidya. It was as if for just their time with me, they would know, and as soon as they left the ashram, amnesia overtook them.

I did not want prati prasav to be a drug that made these people feel better for a little while, but like the Sanjeevani that changes them forever. So I was going through scripture after scripture, trying to discover how to make the prati prasav have a long-lasting impact. One thing is true about theory: no matter how much you study it, there is no substitute for practical learning. You can read book after book on becoming a pilot and still not be able to fly a plane. You can read every book on surgery but still be unable to remove a tumor.

No matter how good a student I was of the theory of prati prasav, Babaji knew that I needed my new teacher to help me learn its practical aspect.

My days were structured around my work, primarily devoted to conducting prati prasav for the visitors who came to us. However, for three hours in the morning and four hours in the evening, I would be with my teacher. These sessions were known as the Brahma muhurta and the Sandhya kala. The Brahma muhurta referred to the early morning hours, typically starting at four o'clock. The Sandhya kala sessions took place in the evening, usually beginning around six and extending until nearly ten at night.

I used to call my teacher Mashe, which means "master." Mashe was quite an enigmatic figure. He spoke a language unfamiliar to me—I did not even know what language it was—and I remained unsure which part of India he came from. Physically, he differed from me; he had a darker complexion and curly hair, and he often adorned his forehead with ashes. He was also much older. Despite his advanced age, Mashe possessed the physique of a gymnast, boasting powerful abdominals and strong, muscular arms with defined triceps. As I conducted prati prasav, I couldn't help but observe him moving around the ashram. He reminded me of a lion pacing in his cage, waiting for food.

The ashram housed *yagashala*, a hall where fire sacrifices took place. From my vantage point at the window, I would watch Mashe as he circled the area with purpose and determination. As evening approached, signaling our time together, he seemed to accelerate, his movements becoming more rapid and focused, like a well-oiled machine, seemingly unaffected by fatigue.

Mashe's dietary habits were unconventional, to say the least. His diet consisted mainly of herbs, which he consumed avidly. I recall one morning watching a man in conversation with the fellow who took care of the greenery, who seemed very downcast.

"Where is that herb that usually grows over there?" the man asked, pointing.

"*Mashe char gaye*," the gardener replied despondently.

Char gaye is a Hindi term that means "grazing," like a cow grazing in a pasture. Mashe's penchant for consuming herbs and his foraging habits often left those responsible for the garden's upkeep frustrated. Mashe would indiscriminately strip trees of their leaves if he found an herb to his liking. In the absence of suitable herbs in the ashram's gardens, he would venture into the forest equipped with a sickle and a *potli* (cloth bag), returning with his finds. On occasion, he would insist that I sample these herbs, presenting them to me in his potli and urging me to partake. Additionally, Mashe utilized these herbs for their healing properties. He had an herb for every use.

Mashe was also known for the sticks he always carried with him. He possessed the skill to fashion any stick into a weapon, regardless of its size. He wielded them with precision, displaying proficiency in their use. When he held a stick, it seemed less like a mere object and more like an extension of his own limb.

Our initial interactions revolved around his instruction in basic yoga practices. We used these foundational practices—asanas—in a very dynamic, fluid style. Even for seasoned practitioners, mastering these postures remains an essential aspect of yoga practice. So in my first meetings with Mashe, he taught me these asanas.

Mashe was also in charge of my meals, and I was restricted to eating only what he provided. I wasn't fond of his cooking, particularly his frequent and lavish use of coconut oil, which had an overpowering aroma. Mashe not only cooked with it but also applied it to his hair, leaving him perpetually scented with coconut.

Sometimes, Mashe would surprise me with a day of just herbs, sparing me from the coconut-oil meals, much to my relief. Other times, he would have me fast for several days, followed by a sudden onslaught of coconut-laden dishes, giving me nausea and vomiting. He would even sometimes insist on fasting for extended periods and then serve rich meals followed by intense yoga sessions, which induced even more vomiting.

Gradually, though, my system adapted. As the days passed, my tolerance increased, and I no longer reacted adversely to Mashe's concoctions. There's an ancient saying among monks that a great yogi is the one who has the power to digest wood and rock. During my time with him, I felt my stomach strengthening, my gag reflex diminishing. I learned to swallow down whatever he offered, viewing it as nourishment rather than a challenge. I took no pleasure in this food, but nor did my body reject it.

I vividly recall a particular day when he served me exceptionally delicious food—fragrant dahl infused with herbs and sweet, semifried balls reminiscent of doughnuts. I had not eaten anything sweet in a long time; sweet things were a luxury, so their taste was especially satisfying—even to someone like me, who had ceased to take pleasure in food. It was a moment of bliss, a reminder of the profound joy a satisfying meal can bring—something you can know only if you have experienced hunger.

Truly, it felt like reaching nirvana, and at that time I felt little enough joy because I was so frustrated from not seeing people benefit from the long-term effects of prati prasav. That day I was especially dejected because I had just come from seeing a young woman I had been working with for almost a month. In India at that time, there was very little health care available, so people would come to the ashram for help: everything from physical ailments to psychological traumas. This young woman was the sweetest, kindest girl you could imagine, but she suffered from PTSD. She was very well educated and had achieved much academic success, getting a scholarship for college. But one day in college, she was the victim of a traumatic incident. Because of that event, she had stomach problems, convulsive hiccupping, and such strong anxiety and panic attacks that she would faint. Because of this onslaught of health problems, she stopped studying and dropped out of college, putting her life on hold. Every day she would come to see me, and we would do a prati prasav session. During the session she would become calmer, but as soon as she opened her eyes, the hiccupping would start once more. Then she would try to breathe deeply and calmly again, but her anxiety would take over, and she would hiccup more and more and more. In a start of sorrow and dejection, she would leave.

After my session with this young woman, I had once again picked up the scriptures to search for a way to help her. I felt so unhappy, so frustrated, asking myself, *Why can't I find a way to make a true difference?*

Later that day, I entered the training hall that had become so familiar to me, but something seemed very different about Mashe. Rather than his customary attire—a simple garment covering his lower body, offset by his oiled skin—he was clad in pristine white robes.

Placing three pots before me, he initiated a profound lesson on unlocking the immortal nature we all have within us. This was a practical lesson in prati prasav, not just theory; a practical in cognitive science, in the system I would go on to develop and that would later be known as the Yoga of Immortals. It began by learning the three *granthis*: points of psychological blockages in the body that obstruct the path to self-realization.

Mashe gestured for me to sit. There was no light in the training room, just an oil lamp in the hall. The lamplight danced, flickering across Mashe's face. Because of the sweat and the oil on his head, he seemed to be glittering like a diamond.

Mashe touched the first pot and then touched his navel. By this he was indicating the Brahma granthi, the first of the three granthis. Then touching the second pot, he touched his heart, indicating the Vishnu granthi. With the third pot, Mashe touched the place where the medulla oblongata connects to the brain, and he said, "Rudra granthi."

Next, Mashe closed his eyes, and I did so too. This was part of our practice: with my eyes closed, I would listen to my teacher as he breathed and match my breath with his breath. Mashe now went through the three granthis again. When he said, "Brahma granthi," he started to breathe in a certain pattern, so I also started to breathe in that manner. In front of me came visions of my emotions, the manas putra of guilt, resentment, and shame. I could see myself and my emotion when I was broken on that day in that stunt, and I could see myself doing the sadhana and becoming better.

Then we changed the breath, and I could feel my consciousness rising. Mashe said, "Vishnu granthi." I took my awareness to the Vishnu granthi, and I could see a vision, and in that vision, I saw the sorrow and the pain that I had in my heart. I could see Rajasthan; I could see losing Shanti. I could see when I was sitting on a chair, broken. I could see the pain that I felt when I was not able to help somebody in prati prasav.

As I gazed on that emotion, and we continued to do the protocol, my consciousness started to rise. And I could see the manas putra: how it changes as the consciousness changes, how shame and guilt become sorrow, how sorrow becomes attachment. As I looked at that attachment, I felt as if I was just about to see what the manas putra looked like at last—because you never get to see the manas putra. It is like a thief who is always wearing a mask; that mask could be any of the emotions, but you never know what it is. As I was about to see its face, our breathing changed, and I could see a great light of the mahasiddhas coming through me and the manas putra dissolving. And as the manas putra dissolved, I could see myself once again having the experience of shaktipat. But this time, I was in control, and I could feel the Shiva.

Just as I was going even deeper, Mashe made a loud noise, and I opened my eyes, annoyed. Why did he pull me out of this amazing spiritual experience? But now, my teacher showed me what lay beneath the third pot. He lifted the pot, and beneath it was the Jyotirlinga—the shivling made of light, the most sacred symbol of divine alchemy, the form of God itself.

When Mashe lifted the pot, he was telling me our goal is not just physical healing, not just to become more spiritual and start to have a following and become a guru yourself. Without words, he was saying, "I want you to focus on the ultimate goal. I want you to be one with the light, which has no age, no gender—it is infinite."

At that time I did not understand: I thought I was near to the finish line, not realizing that a greater goal lay a hundred miles down the road. That day, I was just taking the first steps in my journey to immortality.

Without speaking a word, Mashe had shown me the flow of energy and the breath road map, a practical demonstration of prati prasav. Thankful, I bowed down and touched his feet. That night I kept on reliving that experience, practicing again and again.

The next morning when the young woman came, I felt something was different. She was hiccupping still, her diaphragm spasming. As always, she had a sweet smile on her face, but she looked exhausted. "Sit," I invited her. And we started the process. Just as Mashe had shown me, I guided her awareness to the navel. I told her to follow my breath as I had followed Mashe's breath. The girl started to cry, as she began to relive her experience. I pointed to her heart, and we continued the process. Her emotions became more intense, as if she were a warrior on a battlefield and I were pulling out an arrow from her shoulder: she felt great pain, but after each breath, great relief. This happened again and again, as if thousands of arrows were being pulled from her heart.

As we continued the process, tears kept falling from her eyes. With the sunlight from the window on it, her face glowed. Finally, I pointed to the head and there was silence, and a smile on her face. Even now, I remember her smile: so powerful. After the prati prasav was complete, the young woman opened her eyes. She waited—and her silence was loud. No more hiccups. She was healed. The young woman went running down the stairs and through the ashram: happy, joyous. After so long, she had control of her body once more.

As she was celebrating her healing, I stood watching her. I saw Mashe looking up at me from the yagyashala, waiting for that day's lesson to begin. Suddenly, in my heart was a small tug of dread: *What will he make me do today?* But it was somehow a joyous dread. And I had a few more minutes before I met with him. Enough time to daydream about shaktipat and the path to Shiva.

SAMADHI MEDITATION PRACTICE

Now we invoke your visualization skills.

Sit comfortably, relax, and begin Shiv Yog breathing.

As you inhale, imagine drawing in positivity and life-force energy from your surroundings.

As you exhale, visualize releasing all the light and positivity you have absorbed.

Continue this process.

CHAPTER 14
BREAKING FREE OF OUR MINDS

इच्छा शत्क्तरुमा कुमारी

The power of desire is the goddess, consort of Shiva.

One time, Narada—the greatest devotee of the god Vishnu—went to Vishnu and said, "You are the creator of the universe. Why do you let humanity suffer in their wants? Why don't you fulfill their wishes and let them be content?"

Vishnu looked amused at Narada's question and replied, "Narada, let me show you."

Vishnu took Narada to where a farmer labored in the sweltering heat. Vishnu approached the farmer and said, "Today is your lucky day. I'm here to grant your wish. What do you want?"

The farmer said, "Land, I want land. I work hard on this small piece of land. If I had more, I'd have more crops, and I could be happy."

"It is granted," Vishnu replied. "Run as far as you want, and whatever distance you cover, all that land will be yours. So run until you feel you have enough, but come back and tell me when you feel you have had enough so that I can complete your wish."

It is said Vishnu and Narada waited for a millennium, and the farmer never came back. Never content, always running.

There is an addiction in the run. The world consumes us, engulfing us in a dream: each of us has our own unique dream based upon our experiences. We are stuck in our prisons, always running.

The only thing that will stop us running is if we are forced to stumble. The first time Buddha left his palace, before he became enlightened, he was riding on his chariot when he saw an old man.

"What is that? Can that happen to me?"

Next, he saw a sick man. "What is that? Will it happen to me?"

Then he saw a dead man. "What is that? Can it happen to me?"

Each time his charioteer answered, "Yes—old age, sickness, and death happen to all. My dear prince, it will be your fate too."

That realization awakened Buddha, and he left everything and went into the forest in search of the truth and the supreme reality. Sometimes we need a sharp realization to make us trip while we run so we can reassess who we are, where we are, and where we have to go.

I was running, too, in Dwarka when I got the power of the shaktipat. My avidya ego, my manas putra, the bad wolf inside my mind, drove me to seek approval, appreciation, love from other people. And in my wild run, I tripped and I broke my back. In truth, it was lucky that I broke my back because I was becoming seduced by the world, a slave within my own mind.

When you visit the ancient castles in Rajasthan, you may witness a remarkable sight: elephants carrying visitors on their backs up to the fortresses that lie on the hilltops. These majestic creatures, capable of immense strength, obediently follow the commands of their mahouts, or trainers, who are often very small men.

From a young age, elephant calves are tethered to trees with sturdy chains. Despite their growing size and strength, the young elephants resign themselves to the belief that escape is futile. As the elephants mature, the mahouts replace the chains with flimsy ropes, yet the elephants, conditioned to their perceived limitations, never attempt to break free. Finally, when the fully grown elephant bull is so huge that he has the power to break any chain or uproot any tree, he is still limited in his mind. He does not try to break the chain, and that is how the diminutive mahout controls such a mighty elephant. Ultimately, it is their minds, not their bodies, that are truly bound. And that is why, sometimes, our limitations need to be broken. Only by challenging self-imposed limitations can we truly transcend them and unlock our full potential for immortality.

We confine ourselves within the boundaries of our own minds, and sometimes we need to be startled into awakening. When Suzie and Barbara visited the monastery, they told me the story of Goldilocks, a girl who chased the things that were not too hot or too cold but just right. There is power in "just right" to awaken us and to trip us in our pursuit of more and more. Let's call it the Goldilocks phenomenon.

In Dwarka, I received the shaktipat as I was learning the skills of discipline and the mantras. Those practices were like a dam within me, holding back a magnificent lake of untapped potential. I had barely grazed the power of more and more. With the shaktipat, I was running and running and running, almost lost in the deep sleep of the mind, like an elephant not knowing its own potential. But then I broke my back, and the experience was just right: not too big an injury that it killed me but not too small that I could just brush it off. This pain was just right because it helped me trip and rethink who I am, where I am, and where I want to go.

Lucknow was special for me because it drew me closer to the scriptures with their insights into human cognition, patterns, and self-imposed limitations and because every single day, as I sat with people, guiding them through prati prasav practices, I would see them waking up. What I witnessed reminded me of the way people catch monkeys in India. The monkey catcher comes along with a special pot that has a very narrow mouth, and inside that pot he places some peanuts. Monkeys, as you probably know, love peanuts. The monkey catcher will place that pot out in the open, and the monkeys are drawn by the delicious aroma of peanuts. One of them will squeeze its hand through the narrow mouth and grab some peanuts in its fist. But now, the monkey cannot draw its fist out of the jar. Still, it refuses to let go of those precious peanuts, instead screaming and screaming, "I'm stuck! I'm stuck!" The monkey catcher comes along and takes hold of the monkey, and then simply breaks the pot. If that monkey had just let go of the peanuts, it would be free.

In prati prasav I would see people waking up and really seeing for the first time what they were holding on to. For some it was the pursuit of wealth, for others the desire to be loved or a belief that they were victims of their circumstances. Finally, they could see: "I'm a slave to my run, a slave to my chains." Their consciousness would rise, they would laugh at their own belief system, and at last they could let go and be free, healed, happy.

These fully awakened people would sometimes thank whatever pain they got in their life because it was that pain that led them to Lucknow, to the prati prasav, and to realization. If it had not been for their pain, the "more and more" would never end. In their version of the Goldilocks phenomenon, their pain was the "just right" that had helped them awaken.

Lucknow illuminated for me the principle of learning through experience. It's the application of wisdom in daily life that truly enriches one's understanding. You can learn things by reading about them, but it's only when you see them in action that you truly value them. It's akin to carrying a seed in your pocket all the time, versus planting it and witnessing it blossom into a beautiful flower or a fruit tree. What was once just a dormant seed becomes something that bears fruit and gives life.

I felt privileged to see the seed blossom and bloom in the hearts of people daily. It was like an elephant breaking out from its constraints. Boom! Now it is free, defying the mahout that had ruled its mind.

When we are the elephant or the farmer, we may think a positive thought—but it will not affect us deep down inside because we are so busy, so caught up in doing. Our mind, our soul, each and every single atom, is such a slave to the run, to the more and more, that the positive thought is nothing but a *rangoli*, a design made from petals or sand that will blow away with the first gentle wind. The whole protocol is necessary, repeated practice and practical experience is necessary, for us to take that design deep inside.

I saw this again and again through the thousands of people that went through the prati prasav process. Their consciousness would rise, and they would wake up from their self-induced coma, from their prison of the traumas they had experienced, and then it would be like the awakening of Buddha—the ability to drop the mirage and go toward a higher, more beautiful calling.

Beyond anything else, Lucknow showed me that cure is possible. This is the Sanjeevani, the magic, that Suzie and Barbara were chasing. When I did prati prasav with them, I was just a child; their predicament was psychological and emotional, so I could not really appreciate the cure they experienced. Here in Lucknow, I would see people who were emotionally and mentally abused and scarred.

The only tools I had were prati prasav and Mahakaal, the infinite. But through the prati prasav, I was able to raise people's consciousness from avidya to vidya. Through Mahakaal, I could bring Sanjeevani into people's lives. I would see their emotional wounds healed. After years and years of trauma, they would receive comfort, peace, and joy. After being sucked of all energy by emotional onslaughts, they were rebirthed into a new divine human experience. Each day, as I saw people healing, I became more motivated. And each day, the processes I repeated with other people, I repeated on myself. I could see no limit to the possibilities: if I could be healed and so many people around me could be healed, imagine how powerful this message is for the whole world. Cure is possible.

I didn't care about eating or sleeping. I looked at what the people around me had experienced, and I wanted more of that for myself. I was like Dr. Korotkov, the doctor who had envied the inner bliss and joy we had in the ashram—the difference was that I knew what the source of that bliss was. But I wanted to experience that same energy, that same control, that same power, that same divinity, so I would do those protocols again and again and again.

Once, as I was doing the protocols, deep in meditation, I was taken back to a memory of Rajasthan. In the great hall, two monks were debating about the nature of the world.

"The path to enlightenment is in the Himalayas," one of them said. "Sitting in meditation, resolving each emotion, raising the consciousness, slowly eliminating all that is temporary. When everything that is not Shiva is eliminated, then what remains has to be Shiva."

The other monk did not agree. He pointed around them to the depictions of great siddhas like Buddha. "In this world, you can learn the lessons much faster. You can evolve at a much faster pace and experience detachment from the world. Look at Buddha, whose journey was expedited a thousand times because he was in this world. You can be like a diamond, but instead of taking millions of years to transform from coal to diamond under great pressure, you can achieve enlightenment in one lifetime."

The first monk shook his head. "The world is a double-edged sword. Yes, the spiritual journey can be expedited, but it is only the best of the best, the most blessed, who can go into the world and not be seduced, and then come out the other side shining and awakened."

Just then, I spoke. "I want to go out into this world. I want to experience it." It was just after Suzie and Barbara had been with us, and I was filled with childish glee at the idea.

"You will go, but will you come out the other side?" said the first monk.

And the second monk said, "You will go. And if you come out, you will be the best of us."

As I meditated now, I was struck by his words. I was deep within this world, surrounded by it. The first step was done. The second step: How to come out the other side? How to break the pots? It would take magic. But that was no obstacle: because of Lucknow, I'd started to believe in magic once again.

SAMADHI MEDITATION PRACTICE

Sit, relax, and begin Shiv Yog breathing but this time focusing on exhalation.

With each breath out, visualize yourself releasing all thoughts and emotions that cloud your mind. Feel as though you are letting go of everything within your body—blood, bones, organs—and becoming completely empty.

Meditate on the self as if your skin were a balloon. As you practice Shiv Yog breathing, imagine the balloon expanding with each inhalation and contracting with each exhalation. Continue to breathe and meditate on the vacuum you create inside yourself.

CHAPTER 15

FINDING AN ANCHOR IN CHAOS

उद्यमो भैवर:

Vigorous and continuous effort leads to God.

Every once in a while, I'd venture into the city from the Lucknow ashram. On the outskirts, there were villages with video game parlors, filled with arcade machines. Skilled players, champions of the games, would be deeply engrossed there: navigating through levels, upgrading characters, and immersing themselves in the story. Then there were people like me, utterly clueless! There are two ways to play these games. If you're a skilled player, you jump in and do the adventures. If you don't know how to play, you join as a second player and follow along as the formidable players do everything. You are a nonplayer character, an NPC, just in the background as scenery while the others participate in the adventures. As a second player, your objective is not to get too involved in the action because you will perish. I felt I was tagging along, a puppy following its master, never grasping a game's intricacies. I would try to play the game five times, die five times, and then go back home.

At times in life, I have felt like I did in that arcade—and I do not think I am alone in this. Everyone around me appeared to me like a master player—be it in the monastery in Rajasthan or the ashram in Dwarka or Lucknow. I felt that I had been thrust into an advanced game where others played pivotal roles and I was merely a spectator.

During these moments of disconnection, I pondered on how I could ground myself in order to feel a stronger sense of connection to the world. I felt that my teacher Mashe could see my dilemma. Even though we didn't share a common language, it always seemed that Mashe understood me when no one else could. Initially, I thought my training with Mashe was intended as rehabilitation after my back injury, but before long I realized that our objective was something much deeper. Mashe aimed to align my mind and body, and through truly feeling my body, I would develop the connection I yearned for.

This concept is challenging to explain: How does one feel one's own body? Mashe started to guide me toward awareness as if the body was the key. He would take me through many, many breathwork practices in which I had to focus on my body. I trusted him to lead me into a deeper connection and awareness.

Visitors to the ashram would come to us because they were injured or unwell; we served the role of medical center for them. Mashe could diagnose their ailments with just a glance. His method didn't require him to engage in lengthy discussions and examinations but to observe and intuitively understand. He'd administer his touch, and they'd leave, visibly improved and profoundly grateful. Witnessing these interactions deepened my respect for Mashe, leading me to heed his guidance. As I followed his instructions, a newfound awareness of my body began to emerge.

Our morning training sessions involved learning exercises from the ancient martial arts of Kalari: dynamic movements, inspired by the animal kingdom, focused on the spine's alignment. Mimicking the fluidity of snakes or the strength of lions, these exercises were physically demanding and left me exhausted. When people think of yoga, they may think of it as quite a stagnant activity, like a series of still images. You achieve a form, hold it, then change. Kalari is more like yoga as *wushu*, the art the Shaolin monks practice: more fluid, with more physical impact. Kalari is martial in nature but with no kicking and punching, no intention to strike another. The objective is a dynamic form of meditation where you raise your consciousness and activate your energy centers, making the divine energy flow.

It was the evening sessions with Mashe that targeted not the physical body but the energy body, the *nadis* (channels) and the *granthis* (knots, energetic blockages in the body). These exercises were subtle, gradually raising the energy levels. During and after these sessions, I experienced a heightened state of awareness emerging. At first, it was an awareness of the physical body—the beating of my heart, the breath through my nostrils, the pressing of my teeth on my lips, all kinds of sensations from head to toe. Then this awareness deepened, extending to the internal organs. I could now sense the behavior of my brain, liver, stomach, kidneys. I even felt as though I could influence them.

As I delved deeper into body awareness, I nurtured a deeper rapport with my physical being. It made me ponder: How many of us truly consider our bodies as friends, rather than adversaries? Often, our affections are directed toward our senses—the tongue, the eyes, the ears—rather than toward the entire body and its intricate workings. We seem to be at war with our bodies rather than allied with them. But as my awareness expanded, I began to perceive and even relish the nuances of every cell within me. One day, Mashe brought me a sumptuous meal, laden with sugar. While it pleased my taste buds, I could keenly feel its journey down my esophagus, the subsequent spike in my blood sugar, and the eventual crash as my heart labored to process the sugar.

My newfound hyperawareness had both pros and cons. On the one hand, it grounded me more firmly, affording me a sense of control over my existence. On the other hand, I was becoming aware of my deepest emotions and thoughts. Sometimes we are so numbed by our trauma that we fail to recognize our need for emotional healing. Day by day, my training regimen prompted me to confront my sorrow and anger. So busy had I been trying to learn and fulfill my duties, I didn't realize how angry I was. And the anger I had was toward nothing less than the whole divine realm, which had presented me with such obstacles.

After the training sessions I would do with Mashe, my prati prasav meditations would be very different. Imagine watching a low-resolution video on a laptop, and then watching the same video in IMAX. Every sensation was very strong, almost overwhelming. Emotions from my past would jump to the forefront of my awareness, and I would get scared. Once after a training session, in my meditation I was pulled back into the memory of a time in Rajasthan when I was a very young boy and a visitor gave me a remote-controlled car. We had no electricity and no batteries, so I had no idea how it worked—but it did, and it was the most wondrous thing I had ever seen. One time, Babaji saw me playing with it. Close by was a poor child from one of the nearby villages, playing in the mud. He was playing happily, not crying or upset, but Babaji looked at me and said, "Give that child the toy."

Even at the age of six or seven, I had been taught that my guru's word was law, so I gave my car to that boy. Now, more than a decade later, suddenly I was wailing like a child: "My toy, my car—I lost my car." I didn't even want the car—if someone had handed it to me right then I wouldn't have known what to do with it—but the feeling of its loss exploded inside me, like Romeo losing Juliet. I was so shocked by my outburst: Where the hell did that come from?

I'd never realized it, but in the back of my head somewhere were many lingering *samskaras* or blockages. Over and over again I speculated about my most significant wounds: *Why was my world taken away from me by the flood in Rajasthan? Why did I have to suffer my back injury?* Even the smallest upsets kept coming back to me: *Why was my toy car taken away from me?* I would feel such anger, but I didn't know how to process these emotions, who to blame, or what to do. I could relive these emotions, but the path to release wasn't clear to me.

Because of that, I would carry the residue into my training sessions, and the residue would affect my focus. Especially during the hard martial art exercises of Kalari, I would hurt myself. When I got injured, I wasn't able to train, and without the training, when I did the prati prasav, I wouldn't go as deep. I wouldn't relive a memory, going back to that place and time and experiencing all the sensations; I would just think about it. I became desensitized, in the sense that my newly awakened awareness was numbed once more. Then Mashe would help me heal. Again, I would do the Kalari. Again I would do the prati prasav, see those things, get affected by it, get injured, and then not do the training. Then I would do the prati prasav and just see, not really *feel*, what lay somewhere deep beneath my skin. I was unable to get to it, but I knew it was there, like something submerged in a deep lake. Like the Loch Ness monster, it showed its head once or twice, and I saw it, I experienced it, but then it was gone again, submerged in the depths. And because I was not training now, I couldn't go deep down to that place.

That cycle continued, over and over again. And I could not see the connection between how my effort was helping me go deep down, how my effort was helping me with my prati prasav, and yet my effort wasn't strong enough to break through that wall.

Each setback left me feeling like a player facing an insurmountable boss level in a video game: the hardest challenge of all. Nowadays so many of the games are easy: you can just save and spawn from the last checkpoint. But in the games of the 1990s, if you died you started from the beginning—no respawns, just a relentless cycle of starting over. With each injury, I lamented that all my progress, all the physical effort that I had made, had been in vain because I was not able to overcome this obstacle that sprang from my past and blocked my way forward.

You know, the ancients were truly wise. Remember the tale of amrit manthan, the churning of the ocean for the elixir of immortality? God assumed the form of a turtle, bearing the weight of the mountain, which the celestial beings churned, hoping to extract the precious elixir. But before they could attain amrit, they encountered Halalhala vish, the poison of death. As the poison spread havoc, they called out to Shiva for aid. Shiva came and ingested the poison—but instead of swallowing it, he held it in his throat, turning it blue.

Like the divine beings, I too was working hard on my own amrit manthan, churning the ocean of my emotions. What came up was my own anger, my own resentment, my own sorrow—and it sprang in front of me and blocked my path. This was the vish I did not know how to overcome.

But because of the awareness exercises I was doing, I was being helped in ways that I did not even understand. All these practices made me more grounded in the present moment. When you are aware and grounded, then through your body Shiva talks, and you have the ability to listen, if you choose.

One such time occurred when I was sitting beneath a tree with Tufan lying beside me. In my cycle of training, I had once again gained the state of hyperawareness, and I was sitting in the shade of the tree, just breathing. Abruptly, one of Tufan's ears stuck straight up in the air like an antenna. Next, both ears pricked and swiveled in the same direction. He lifted his head and gazed intently at something. In the line of his gaze, I saw a child with a ball in his hand. The child threw the ball in the sky. Tufan's eyes were glued to the ball as it went up, and then came back down. Up and down, the child threw the ball, and Tufan's eyes never left it. Just as Tufan's eyes were connected to the ball, so my breath became connected to the ball. The ball flew up, up, up, and I was inhaling. Suddenly, the ball could go no higher, and I could inhale no more. The ball started to descend, and I exhaled—out, out, out. Again, the child threw the ball up: the child's force was applied to the ball. Then the Earth's gravity was applied to the ball, and it fell down.

I realized that I was like that ball being pushed up and down. When life pushed me to live, I inhaled; and when mortality called me, I exhaled. In that moment, Tufan's eyes and the ball and I were connected. Then a thought struck me: *When is the ball free?* I started to notice that there comes a moment, a mere millisecond, when the ball has risen as high as it can, and yet the Earth has not yet started pulling the ball down. For that one millisecond, the ball is free from the boy's force and the Earth's force. What if, I wondered, we could increase that time, that moment? And I started to meditate on that point. I knew that if I continued the cycle of hyperawareness, eventually my anger and my resentment would rise up. This vish would be everywhere, and I would not be ready to face it. Not having enough divinity, not having the Shiva to drink the poison, it would kill me once again. And I would have to start the video game all over again. But what if I could somehow remain in this instant of freedom and not let the anger come?

This time, when the ball went up, I inhaled, and as the ball went down, I exhaled—but my focus was not on the inhalation and the exhalation. Now, my focus was on the point in between ascent and descent, in between inhaling and exhaling. As I started to meditate on this point, it was as if everything was suddenly in slow motion. I could see the ball frozen in the sky. I could see Tufan's eyes, I could see the ants gathering food, I could see the bees flying from flower to flower, I could see the birds making their nests, I could see the trees breathing. Every living being was just doing what they did, and I thought, *So will I*. In that suspended moment, I felt strong, aware, connected.

It was the most remarkable meditation—right up until the point when the boy dropped the ball and Tufan ran like the wind to snatch it up, startling the boy so much I thought he might soil his pants.

I have an anchor, I realized, a steady point amid life's tumultuous currents.

That evening, I sought out Mashe. His gaze seemed to pierce through me, as if sensing something new within me. He motioned for me to commence the training, directing me toward the *meypayattu*: the backbone of Kalari training, a set of physical practices that imparts strength to the body and the mind and makes the student sure-footed. These intricate sequences of movements are akin to a choreographed dance, graceful yet formidable, something like *surya namaskar*, the sun salutation you may know from yoga. As I began, the familiar surge of hyperawareness engulfed me, and I sensed the impending arrival of anger, lurking in the shadows. I knew that the moment it touched me, I would become weak, I would lose myself; I would make mistakes, and I would fall.

But now, I had a newfound tool at my disposal. Instead of succumbing to the onslaught of emotions, I focused on the space between breaths, slowing time itself. Now, rather than the inhalation and the exhalation and the anger, I took my awareness to the point in between the breath, and everything started to go in slow motion. At first it was for a second. I saw the anger come a little bit closer. Then it was for a few minutes. And I saw the anger come closer. And then suddenly, I was in that zone, and the only thing that was moving was my body. Under Mashe's unwavering gaze, so much like Tufan's watchful eyes, I freed myself. I was like that ball in the middle of the sky, not affected by the boy or the Earth. As I meditated on the space between my breath, I found myself in a place beyond thoughts. I finished the meypayattu, and the anger edged a little closer to me again.

"Again."

Mashe is looking at me, and I am utterly thrown off balance. After one and a half years, he finally speaks to me in a language I know! I am so confused; I'm thinking, *What the hell!* And the anger creeps closer. *Oh no, no, no,* I tell myself. I focus on the moment between breath, and I stop time. As soon as I finish the meypayattu, Mashe repeats the word.

"Again."

I can feel the sweat on my brow, but it doesn't fall because I am like that ball in the sky, in an in-between place. Not alive, not dead. No gravity or force. Just me. Somewhere in between, like the space between atoms. The sweat does not fall; I do not lose my breath.

"Again."

I do it again and again and again, and I'm tired—I can see exhaustion coming upon me from a distance, standing at the door with the anger. But I have stopped time, I reason, so I cannot be tired.

"Again."

In all my life I had never done the meypayattu more than two or three times. That day, I don't know how many times I did them. With each repetition, I felt a surge of energy, the *kundalini shakti*, the divine energy of Shakti rising up from the base of my spine. As I continued the meypayattu, I could feel a power I had never felt before; it was as if I were becoming hotter and hotter and hotter, like the surface of the sun.

And just when I thought the world must explode, Mashe said, "Again."

I continued and I continued, and finally when I looked at my hands, I could not see my flesh; all I could see was pure, bright light.

When I looked up, Mashe was smiling. Now I focused not on his eyes but his face. And instead of Mashe, I saw Shiva standing in front of me. As soon as I saw Shiva—boom, the ball fell down! Time became normal again. I lost awareness of my breath, and I saw the anger come closer and closer. I couldn't do anything; I just looked at Shiva, and from somewhere inside me emerged a small prayer that simply said, *Help*. And just as Shiva drank the poison of the universe, Shiva came between me and that anger. And somewhere within Shiva, the anger disappeared.

As the anger drained away, Shiva smiled and said, "Again."

I found my breath, and I started to focus again on the point in between the breath. I had a sudden realization that you do what you need to do: your dharma. Irrespective of the rain, the ant collects food; irrespective of the wind, the bee makes its hive; irrespective of the sun, the bird sings. So, I must do what I must do, irrespective of what had happened in my life. As I did the meypayattu again and again, focusing on the breath, I realized that no matter how adverse the elements may seem, they enable the seeds to germinate; they help the bird find its way; and I am where I am because of what has happened in my life.

It was only now I could realize this, because for the first time I could go beyond the anger.

I do not know how many times more I did the meypayattu, but finally I sat down and closed my eyes, and I felt for the first time in my life that I wasn't in somebody else's video game. This was my video game; I was the main player. I was utterly aware of my body and everything that existed around me.

In that moment, I started the prati prasav protocol. As I did so, there was so much energy inside me. For the first time, I could project that power and penetrate through those emotions of guilt and shame and anger. Through this energy, I could relive the emotions—and release them. I could feel the consciousness flowing up, the coiled-up energy flowing up my spine. It was the kundalini shakti: the serpent rising. I had never felt such a thing before: all the way from my navel and up through my heart, something so powerful, so divine, it was very close to the experience of shaktipat.

Now, the same memories came to me, but they had lost their emotional charge. I could see myself giving away the toy car, but I wasn't angry anymore. I was happy. I could see all the things that had happened, but each memory was without emotional weight: instead, I felt a calm, collective acceptance of everything that had happened. For the first time, I felt as if I had gone beyond the emotions and I felt lighter, as if many arrows had been pulled out of my body.

In that state of divine awareness, I opened my eyes, and I saw Mashe smiling.

For the first time I had seen the correlation: awareness had brought me wisdom. Wisdom had given me motivation to work hard, to do the protocols. The protocols had given me the power I needed to churn myself in the prati prasav sadhana, and the prati prasav sadhana had given me that purification, the higher consciousness.

Because I understood this cycle, every day from then on was different. Every day I worked harder on my Kalari. Every day I worked harder on the prati prasav sadhana. Every day a smile grew on my face.

One day I went to the yagashala with a smile, ready for anything Mashe might throw at me.

But that day I did not see him walking like a lion. He was sitting happily, quite relaxed. A relaxed Mashe was something I'd never seen. I smiled. He smiled back, and he told me in a language I could understand, "My work with you is done."

As he said it, he threw his stick like the divine weapon of Vishnu, and he broke the first pot, the one that represented the Brahma granthi.

I hugged him, and the Shiva within him who had shown me my true nature, my capability, my power. With much love, I blessed and thanked Mashe and bid him farewell.

After Mashe left, I sat with Tufan in front of the statue of Mahakaal. As I stared at the two remaining pots, the Vishnu and the Rudra, I wondered, *What will I do with my breath?* Most of all, though, I was secure in the knowledge that I now possessed the tools to navigate life's challenges, with my body and breath as steadfast companions.

SAMADHI MEDITATION PRACTICE

Sit comfortably, relax your body, and meditate on the sun. Imagine the sun as a friend, embodying all the positivity, divinity, and strength you need.

Inhale for a count of three, feeling the sun's light flow into your head and through your entire body.

Exhale for a count of three, releasing everything from your body through your head and into the sun.

One, two, three—inhale deeply; three, two, one—exhale fully.

Repeat this cycle for ten minutes, keeping your breath as deep and powerful as possible.

CHAPTER 16

TWO BIRDS IN A TREE

विद्यासमुत्थाने स्वाभाविकेखेचरी शिवावस्था

By raising knowledge inherent in oneself, one reaches the highest state of consciousness, which is the state of Shiva.

One day in Lucknow, someone borrowed a portable DVD player and a copy of the movie *Les Misérables* with Liam Neeson playing Jean Valjean. Six of us sat together to watch the movie on a tiny screen, and I was blown away by the power of the performance, the emotion of the story. I leapt up, ready to give a standing ovation. Then I looked around and saw the other five with their mouths open and eyes closed, deep in slumber, snoring.

It is amazing how different each human is from one another. I was taught that just as each of us has a dominant hand, each of us has a dominant sense. We perceive the world according to our dominant sense. You can see this in the way people pray. Somebody whose dominant sense is hearing will sing to the glory of God. Somebody whose dominant sense is seeing will draw the most glorious images of God. Somebody whose dominant sense is smell will use incense and fragrances to connect to the divinity. In India, somebody whose dominant sense is taste will prepare *chappan bhog*, fifty-six dishes in the name of God. Each person thinks their path to divinity is the ultimate one. Likewise, every human being, according to their dominant senses and their past experiences, perceives the world in a different way.

My job was to bring people to prati prasav because, after Mashe, I really believed cure was possible. I wanted people to experience the healing that could happen when they go deep down through the process of prati prasav—the healing that I had experienced—so I would try to take people on that journey. But even though we are all the same species—*Homo sapiens*—we are completely different from one another in the most unexpected ways. Some people, like me during *Les Misérables*, would have phenomenal, life-changing experiences; others were like my five companions, snoring with their mouths open. I was confused. Why does this happen?

Reflecting on my time in various monasteries with various monks, I saw that there was so much difference between the outcomes of each and every monk's effort to seek the divine, and I pondered even more. If there is any mathematical logic to the world, why is it that when we are applying the principles of prati prasav, we add two plus two and sometimes we get four and other times we get onety-one? Not even eleven—onety-one! At first I thought it was a little like when you buy medicine, and on the label it's written: "Some people may experience itchiness, dizziness, or diarrhea. If you have these symptoms, consult your physician." Perhaps prati prasav was like that, with the power to heal but equally able to cause discomfort or have no effect at all.

I would feel profoundly connected when someone found healing through the process of prati prasav. As the Brahma granthi, my energetic blockages, had opened up in me, I found I was changing, with a new longing for such connection. Empathy and compassion grew in me daily, but alongside them was confusion about why some people gain so much and others hardly anything. My curiosity swelled into a passion, an obsession: How could I find the pathway into a person's heart so they could feel the same bliss that I experienced?

It was at that time I got an invitation to meet with my father. It came at an interesting time for me, because I had been doing therapy with so many people and I had started to understand what this concept of a "father" meant for other people: someone who played ball with them, hugged them, made sure their clothes were neat and they had food in their stomach. It was very different from my relationship with my father. And so, with this meeting I had expectations.

However, you know that my father was a siddha. *Siddha* literally means "perfection." My father, the monks I met in the monastery, Mashe—all of them were siddhas, the ones who have become connected to the immortal self, free from the shackles of attachment and life itself.

The siddhas don't ascribe to karma. They lean toward dharma. Karma is being born to settle your past debts. A siddha is born not to settle their past debts but to fulfill their duty—their dharma. Their duty is to assist the people who are on a spiritual journey. Even for the siddha, it has taken many lifetimes to reach where they are, so a siddha understands the struggle. Through their compassionate nature, they help those who are on the path.

And so my siddha father had called me to him. I got very excited because I had not seen him since I started my work with Mashe. At the same time, I had all these newly developed concepts of a father from my work with people in prati prasav. How a father would be to his child, and the expectations of a child from their father. I was thinking of all these things, and I was making all these scenarios in my head: *When I meet with my father, I'll say this and do this.*

By this time, my father had become extremely famous in India as a master who had come into the light to guide people. A lot of wise men don't share their knowledge; my father was renowned because he was accessible, and he would teach without discrimination, traveling around the country to reach as many people as possible. Men and women, people of all denominations would come to him to learn. So there was always a crowd of people around him and a very mystical aura surrounding him. He was a phenomenon.

Probably for that reason, he always chose to stay near a city, but never in a city, in a place that could accommodate a large gathering. This time, I was called to one of his ashrams to meet him. It was in the city outskirts, a rural area surrounded by wilderness. We kept on driving and driving until eventually we came to a dirt road, and at the end of that dirt road was a small complex. And in that complex, my father was staying. The complex was filled with many people who had come to meet him. When I was brought into the room where my father was, I saw him sitting on his chair at the front, with a group of people in front of him.

My heart was racing so hard I could hear each heartbeat thumping in my chest. I was walking as if I were the king of the world, a prince returning out of exile. Everybody could see I was different, I was sure. Nobody there knew I was his son, but there must surely be an aura of grandeur around me; something that told the world I was special. I was thirsty for love, for acknowledgment, to be noticed. I had never experienced a father, in the traditional sense. I had only experienced a guru. And now, even though I was a grown-up person, this thought was in my head: how good it would be to be loved like a son by his father. Everyone in that hall was getting my father's attention, but I thought it would be good if I could be loved just a little bit more than anybody else.

I sat down, waiting to be treated in a special manner. My father kept on talking to people. *Maybe he hasn't noticed his son is here*, I was thinking. *He should look over here!*

One hour passed, then two hours, and it was almost evening. I was starting to get uncomfortable. And then finally he looked at me. And he said, "Ishan! Come here." I suddenly became very proud. *Yes! He has called me; he knows that I've overcome my Brahma granthi, and I now have so many spiritual powers, and I have this understanding of my body and this and that and... that I'm better than everybody who's sitting here.*

As I stood, I got caught up looking at everybody around me. *Yeah, see? I told you, I'm awesome!*

"Ishan, come here."

I went to him, and he said, "Ishan, I have a job for you."

Muscle memory kicked in, for I had been trained all my life into obedience. I nodded and waited for my guru's command.

"Take Shambho out for a walk."

"Shambho?" I asked him, nonplussed. "Who the heck is Shambho?"

"Here, go with this man." He indicated someone standing nearby. "He will show you Shambho."

I went with the gentleman out behind the hall. There stood the biggest bull that I had ever seen. It had huge horns, and it looked so strong, as if he could just barrel through any place and turn it into dust if he wanted.

"This is Shambho," the gentleman told me.

I craned my neck to look up at the bull. Beside him, I was tiny. Nervously, I took hold of the rope that was tied to his neck. I started to walk, and to my amazement Shambho followed along, entirely docile. He was just chewing his cud, looking as though he was chewing gum all the time. Shambho was just relaxing, chilling, and when I walked, he walked.

I went out of the complex into the surrounding wilderness. I kept on thinking, *Why wasn't I treated like someone special? I'm his son!* In my time giving therapy, I'd learned that parents spend their lifetimes taking care of their children, so I was a bit upset that the first thing my father did when he saw me was to give me a menial job. He didn't even ask me how I was! I could have been in pain. Of course, I wasn't—I was perfectly well. And he had found me Mashe, who had shown me the path so I could heal myself. But there was this persistent thought in my head: *Why didn't he seem to care?*

I was walking and walking, and the bull was walking behind me, and I kept on thinking, becoming more than a little upset. Sadness has this magic: it makes time go slowly. It is like quicksand. You sink in it, and then you're stuck in time, preserved in your gloom. In Alaska, there is a bison from the Ice Age: Blue Babe, they call it. During the Ice Age, it got stuck in the snow and its body was mummified. After tens of thousands of years, a gold miner stumbled across its perfectly preserved body. With sadness it is the same: you get stuck in a certain thought. Even after ten thousand years, you are there thinking about that one thing. Luckily for me, it wasn't ten thousand years—in fact, it was about one and a half hours.

As the sun started to set, I looked around me and realized I was utterly, thoroughly, profusely lost. There was no road. There were just trees. Remember, this is the Indian wilderness, where there are leopards, snakes—even gangs seeking to dump a body in a swamp. And I was alone with Shambho in that wilderness. As soon as I realized that I was lost, I got agitated. I started to run around. Even in my panic I realized Shambho, that gentle giant, was not panicking. His eyes were still tranquil, and he was still chewing away amiably. This was most annoying; I wanted Shambho to be frantic like me. So I pulled the damn bull along, dragging it here and there. For fifteen or twenty minutes, I ran around trying to get my bearings. I tried to climb a tree to figure out where I was, but all I could see was wilderness. As the sun set and evening started to draw in, I lost hope. I thought, *This is it. I'm in the wilderness with a bull. The bull is big and strong. I'm not, and I don't know what's going to happen to me.* I gave up and prepared to die.

But now a change happened. When I left the complex, I was walking in the front and the bull was in the back. But now Shambho was walking in front and I was behind him, gazing at my feet, thinking of all the things that could happen to me, stuck there in the wilderness.

After some time following the bull, I looked up and I saw the ashram complex. I threw my arms in the air. "Hurray! I'm saved!" I looked at the bull, and the bull looked at me, surely thinking I was crazy. But the truly crazy thing was I had traversed such peaks and valleys of emotion in the last two hours—excited, sad, scared, then excited once more. All this time Shambho had been calm, at ease, and content. For me, it was my first time in the forest, but the bull had walked on this path a thousand times. Shambho knew the way.

When I got back to the complex, I tied the bull behind the building. I could hear my father talking to some people gathered inside. He was telling them a story from the Upanishads—ancient books passed down through spoken word, before written history existed.

"Our mind is like two birds on a tree," my father said. "One is a silent bird, sitting on the highest branch of a tree, observing the second bird. The second bird is loud and agitated, jumping from branch to branch. The second, agitated bird is our conscious self, and the first bird that is observing is our wise subconscious."

I listened and I started to connect my father's story with what had happened with me. I saw myself as the agitated bird jumping from branch to branch, and Shambho as the wise observer who did not need to be agitated at all. He knew the way—the way back home.

That is the crazy thing about siddhas: their teachings are not like a recipe book. How easy spirituality would be if it could be taught like a recipe book! Do this, then that, in this quantity, that quantity. The teachings of siddhas are more like a riddle: a complex, poetic riddle. The riddle is out in the open for anyone to see, like an apple tree; even so, it can be deciphered only by a wise few, like Isaac Newton sitting under his apple tree.

My father kept on speaking. I sat there and listened, and as he continued his story, he paused for a moment. He just looked at me and he said, "Shambho."

Shambho was the name of the bull. Shambho is also another name for Shiva. Now, I could see that Shambho was the wise subconscious, and I knew that Shambho was the way back home.

SAMADHI MEDITATION PRACTICE

Close your eyes, sit comfortably, and relax your body.

Visualize your god, the supreme being, as a form of divine energy in front of you.

Focus on your heart, seeing it as a gateway into your body.

As you inhale for a count of three, imagine the light of the supreme being flowing from your heart into your body. As you exhale for a count of three, surrender yourself through your heart to the supreme being.

Inhale for a count of three, then exhale for a count of three. With each breath, meditate on the idea that with each inhalation, you become less of yourself and more of God.

Continue this practice for fifteen minutes.

CHAPTER 17
FALLING IN LOVE WITH SHIVA

अभिलाषाद् बहिर्गतिः संवाह्यस्य ।

Due to desire for external objects, an individual is carried from life to life.

Are we bound by our past deeds? This is the concept of karma as it is known in the West and in some traditional Eastern philosophies. This form of karma theory says that positive thoughts, words, and actions are rewarded by positive consequences; negative thoughts, words, and actions are met with negative consequences. However, in my tradition, the siddha tradition, I was taught that the burden of karma exists only because we are in a deep sleep. When we wake up, we raise our consciousness, and we see that the bondage is an illusion. Now that we are awake, there is no attachment—and when there is no attachment, there is freedom. There is no need to strive for thousands of years, through many lifetimes, to resolve every single action. Instead, you do the sadhana practice and you become free.

Think of the difference between the karma perspective and the siddha perspective like this. When you drive a car, all the driving laws, every curve in the road, every pothole will affect you. Your thoughts are consumed with *Do I take this turn? Must I stop at this intersection? Which side of the road should I be on?* (A very important question for drivers in foreign countries!) When you are traveling in a plane, all those questions are irrelevant, and you are free from them. The way you reach your destination is different, and your vantage point is transformed.

Karma or not, many of us live as though our past actions are our eternal prison. Our anger, fear, hurt, and grief all restrict and define our actions in the present. An awakening is needed here too.

Prati prasav awakens people from their deep sleep. I saw many people connect to the Shambho, the divine self, through prati prasav. They would see the absurdity in their previous attachments, and their nature would change.

And yet this was not true for everyone, and this puzzled me greatly. I worked with other people for whom prati prasav was not accessible. Because of their dominant senses and their past experiences, they could not connect to their divine self through prati prasav.

Someone who has never meditated before needs to undergo preparation, like tilling a field before planting the seeds. I realized that the sequences I learned from Mashe could be a precursor to the deeper prati prasav process. Yogis had used these techniques from time immemorial to bring them into a certain state. Later, they became the building blocks for the system I would call Yoga of Immortals. I simply found ways to organize these ancient practices so that anyone could do them. Some of them are the samadhis in this book.

When I was young, kids used to tell a joke that goes like this. In a marketplace, a man was selling Chinese fans—the kind that you hold in your hand and wave to create a cooling breeze. He told every customer, "This fan will work for one hundred years, and I even give a one-hundred-year guarantee."

One man who came to his stall bought this Chinese fan with the one-hundred-year guarantee, brought it home, and almost immediately it broke. So he went back to the seller.

"You said this fan would work for one hundred years, but it broke in less than a day! How could you be so foolish to claim that this flimsy fan would last a long time?"

"No, you are the foolish one," the seller replied. "It's a special fan, so there is a special technique to use it. You don't wave the fan back and forth—you hold it in front of your face and move your head from side to side. *Then* it will work for one hundred years!"

Sometimes meditation teachers and yoga teachers whose method is not working with their students will say that the method is fine; the student is just doing it wrong. User error!

My father sent me back home with an encrypted message: *Shambho*. Shiva. But I was seeing that some people could not connect to Shambho. I knew it was not those students' fault; there was no user error. With my whole heart, I longed to find a way that people might have the desire and ability to connect to Shambho.

My job had always been very simple: to help people go from avidya to vidya, to move from lack of knowledge to knowledge. They had always been walking with Shambho, as I walked with the bull; the higher self is always within us. But we have abused the bull so much: trying to push it, conquer it, make it do what we think it should do. Too rarely have we taken counsel from our higher self;

too rarely have we have gone within, connected, and listened to the voice of our divine self. My job was to clean people's minds, just as a cleaner would sweep a house to make it habitable. Once the mind was habitable, a person's higher self could take over. Once the vidya is there, they do not need me to cleanse so intensively. After that, they might need me if they get stuck; but now there will be a love affair that is going on in their hearts with Shiva. It will be a living system.

I have told you about the time I came across a bear in the woods and I froze. But that was a "happily ever after" fairy-tale version rather than the full story. Now, let me tell you everything.

One day I was walking far in the wilderness and in front of me I saw a cute little baby bear. He was so delightful that immediately my heart was filled with love and joy, and I decided that I would take care of that orphan baby. If I could care for a hyena, why not a helpless bear cub? As I was gazing with adoration at that little bear, lost in my plans to adopt him, suddenly, I saw in front of me a gigantic mama bear. That bear loomed over me and let loose a mighty roar of anger.

At that moment I realized that what I had learned in textbooks was wrong. They used to say that when you see something that causes you enormous fear, there is a fight-or-flight reaction. What I experienced was what more modern textbooks call freeze. I looked at the bear, and I was paralyzed. I forgot I was a great martial artist—as if it mattered. Would I do kung fu with the bear? I forgot I was a monk—in any case, would I chant mantras with the bear? I forgot I was a yogi—who cares? Was I going to do downward dog position with the bear? I simply froze before the angry mama bear in front of me.

The only thing that came in my head was the phrase Babaji had said to me in Dwarka and many times since: *Shiv, Shivanand, Shiv Yogi.* Shiv means the great infinite power; Shivanand means the guru; and Shiv Yogi means the disciple. This phrase expresses the trust a student must have that he is walking on the right path. So I said out loud, "Shiv, Shivanand, Shiv Yogi." And from that phrase, I got power. I got energy. I got wisdom. And the wisdom that I got—even though bear experts will disagree on my strategy—was to *run*. So I did: I ran as fast as I could, and in my head I was repeating, *Shiv, Shivanand, Shiv Yogi. Shiv, Shivanand, Shiv Yogi. Shiv, Shivanand, Shiv Yogi.* I didn't even look back to see if the bear was chasing me; I ran and ran and ran. And the only thing that was pushing me to run was hope and trust—trust that the student always has the divinity and strength within him.

Suddenly, there and then, it clicked. I trusted the divinity to save me from the bear, and that thought gave me the power to run like the wind. So I ran! And the bear could not catch me.

Then I thought to myself, *What if there was no trust? What if there was no hope?* I would have remained frozen, and the bear would have eaten spicy food: me. I don't know what I really taste like, but I assume I would be spicy.

When I was lost in the forest with the bull Shambho, I'd given up and I had no hope; that was why I followed Shambho to the path. But it struck me that what Babaji had been trying to tell me was that I must find trust and hope in the higher self, to Shambho, *before* anything else—even before the prati prasav.

From that day onward I started to spend a little bit more time with the people who came to me for the prati prasav therapy. I started to make an effort so that they would enjoy and appreciate—even love—the process. I would do satsang with them, and I would tell them stories about Shiva. No matter how impenetrable our defenses are, sometimes a story can find its way into our heart. Then the story explodes, deep inside us.

Before, I had been treating the prati prasav like an assembly line where one person comes, then another and another. Because it was a purely mechanical process without involvement of the heart, the people who did not succeed failed because they did not have hope, or they did not trust the process. And the people who succeeded? Somehow, somewhere deep down, they had love: for the monks, for the monastery, for Shambho—Shiva. Only because there was such love, they could go through the process. Now, I realized that to make sure the prati prasav was successful, I needed to bring the people together, to love Shambho—before I gave therapy.

The beautiful thing about humanity is we learn from one another. I used to take the prati prasav one person at a time because I thought the spiritual path was a very solitary path; I thought you had to be alone with yourself—in a cave, on a mountain, under a tree. Now I realized I was missing the community factor. After all, I myself am never alone. Even when I am on a mountain, in a cave, or under a tree, through my breath it is always Shiv, Shivanand, Shiv Yogi. The god, the guru, and the student are always walking together.

There is something amazing about the way people get inspiration from one another. If within a crowd, there is one person who has discovered their Shambho—who has grown, evolved, ascended, and healed—that person automatically creates hope in another person. And the more that person sees others benefiting and rising, the more effort they put into their own sadhana samadhi, and the more their love for their god awakens. Without that feedback of seeing people a little further ahead on the journey, there is always a sense of doubt. It's like when we see an advertisement showing us people who have attained a certain state—enjoying a Snickers bar, perhaps!—we say, "I can see myself there."

As I brought people together to do prati prasav, the people in our group who could release and let go would become an inspiration for those who were frozen in their fears. Maybe today, they would not let go; maybe tomorrow, they would not let go. But now at least they saw that letting go was possible, and one day there would be a breakthrough. This acceptance, this hope, from seeing others blossoming like a flower—when it came inside people's hearts, they started to change. They began to understand, commit, loosen, relax, open up to the whole process. The mystery was gone: before they may have thought, *A guru will come in the room, and the prati prasav will happen, and then happily ever after—the end.* But now it was all out in the open, no more fairy tales. There was a whole community growing together, working together, healing together, falling in love with Shiva together.

When the communities started to thrive, the chain reaction became unstoppable. It's like a fusion reaction: it just needs heat and a push to make a collision happen, so that the atoms fuse and release their energy. Now imagine divinity, hope, trust, and love spreading from one person to another, a holy ripple through the waters of the world. One person heals and changes; then immediately in the vicinity of that person, someone else gets inspired—and so on and so forth. When you see such a chain reaction, you know it is a form of immortality: the divine within us, never-ending.

Hope and trust are great motivators, it is true. But the question is: How do we attain hope and trust? There has to be divine love, binding all.

Unless we take counsel with our higher self, we are frozen like a deer in the headlights, or a boy in the woods with a bear. But it is with hope, trust, and love that we make that Herculean effort. It is in that effort that you connect to the deepest, most powerful form of yourself—and miracles happen.

At the time of our greatest crisis, we are open to the greatest change, if we make that effort. But to overcome our inertia, the force we need is the hope, the trust, and above all divine love.

The higher self, the inner Shambho, has the power. That is the truth of the saying, "You are the creator of your own destiny." Through your hands, you can write your destiny. You can write your own path.

As the community grew, the granthi of the heart started to dissolve among us. This granthi, this blockage, can dissolve only when there is love. It is amazing how big we can make our hearts if we want to, and how much we can fit in our hearts. The mahasiddhas say the universe is within us. But to fit the universe within the self, love must spread and encompass the universe.

One day, there was a loud commotion. Everyone looked around, and I asked someone near me, "What happened?"

"Oh, Shambho the bull got out," they told me.

I went to see where Shambho had gone. Maybe by chance, or maybe by destiny, Shambho had gotten into the training hall, and he had broken the second pot—the one that represented the Vishnu granthi of the heart, emotional attachment, the second of the three pots that were placed there by Mashe. Shambho was sitting beside the broken pot, looking at me. Still chewing his cud, still calm, still relaxed as ever, he seemed to gesture with his head toward the third and final pot, as if to show me that I was ready for that final step.

I knew that the time had come to continue my journey. No matter how much I now loved Lucknow, no matter the wonderful community I had made there, it was time for me and Tufan to move on to the next chapter. The unknown. But what could go wrong? After all, I had love, hope, and trust.

SAMADHI MEDITATION PRACTICE

Inhale deeply, and as you exhale, chant the mantra *om* loudly for as long as you can.

Direct the sound to the top of your head. Feel the vibration moving from your head and spreading throughout your body.

As you chant, sense the vibration resonating in every cell of your body.

Repeat this process eleven times.

CHAPTER 18
CHASING THE IDEA OF SPIRITUALITY

सोऽहं हंसा शिवा

I am the swan that rises to merge with Shiva.

Sometimes you can help a multitude of people, yet not receive the same help yourself. Think of a physician who gives all their energies and attention to their patients, but has no one to show them the same care and attention. Or a talented musician, who pours every emotion into their performance, only to find themselves depleted at the end. Even more than that, health workers and therapists may find that as the people they care for evolve and drop their negativity, sometimes a dark residue is left with the person who is helping them.

In my spiritual journey, I hadn't yet reached the highest point; I wasn't one with the infinite energy. In my finite capacity I was helping the people who came to me in the best way I could, but their residue was being left with me, layer after layer. Even though I was doing my meditations and protocols with great dedication, I would sometimes get affected by this residue. I would see these people reaching the highest of divine energies, and I would think, "They have reached these heights because I'm holding their hand and helping them. If only someone would hold *my* hand so I could reach the heights."

Long ago, there lived a great monk in our monastery named Sumedha Maharshi. He and all of his students were enlightened. They not only had great intellectual knowledge, but they also had an intricate understanding of the world and the workings of all matter.

One day, there was a king who had lost everything to his rivals in battle. In exile, roaming through the forest on his horse, he came upon the monastery. There was also a merchant who had been thrown out of his house by his wife, who had plotted with her lover to take everything the merchant had. He was aimlessly wandering in the forest, and he too stumbled upon the monastery.

Sumedha Maharshi took them both in and trained them how to overcome their own selves and how to ascend to enlightenment—or at least walk the spiritual path. What this great monk provided to the king and the merchant was something of a master class in psychology, conveyed through stories about the divine goddess Shakti. Sumedha Maharshi told them about how Shakti had to get rid of many demons so that there could be light. These demons represent our psychological afflictions: among the demons are Dhumra Lochana, which literally means "fog in front of the eyes" and indicates depression; Raktabija, which symbolizes our never-ending thirst for materialistic pleasures; and Apasmara, which represents spiritual ignorance. As we evolve and rise higher, the qualities of the demon we are slaying change.

In the end, Shakti overcomes them all. Sumedha Maharshi

explained to the king and the merchant: "Just as the goddess overcame these demons, you have to overcome your afflictions, and then you'll be free."

He taught them meditation, and both the king and the merchant overcame their afflictions, one by one. Once they were one with the light, Sumedha Maharshi asked them both, "What do you want?"

"I want revenge," the king replied. "I cannot be at peace till I get rid of the tyrant king who is ruling my kingdom. I want to learn the secrets of Shakti so I can go back and use them to regain power."

"All my life I worked hard to create my business and support my wife, and I was thrown away as if I didn't even exist," the merchant replied. "Now, I just want to know, Why am I here? What's the point of this life? I have experienced a little joy and bliss in sadhana, but now I want to experience the greatest joy of samadhi. That's why I wanted to learn from you—I want to go deeper and merge with the infinite."

Sumedha Maharshi blessed them both. And it is said that the merchant continued his practice and became a great monk himself, while the king took what he had learned and used it to his own material advantage, returning to his pursuit of power and reaching even higher levels than before his exile.

To a certain point, the king won the battle with his Apasmara, but only until he reached a level where he found comfort and satisfaction. The king didn't see any problem with this: he was content with where he had reached. But the merchant had tasted divinity. He had started to understand the illusion of this world, the transient nature of existence. He wanted nothing less than the ultimate prize, the greatest gift. So the merchant worked to eliminate all samskaras, finally overcoming the Apasmara in its entirety.

Many of the people who came to the monastery were like either the king or the merchant. Some, like Suzie and Barbara, came there to learn just what they wanted to learn and then take it back to their world and use it in whatever way they saw fit. Even after achieving so much tranquility and bliss, there was still an objective they had in mind, which would eventually creep its way back into their intentions. Then there were those like the merchant, who were done with the materialistic life and mortal constraints and did not wish to return to that life. They did not want to settle for anything less than divinity.

When people came to the monastery, some did not stay with us long before they wanted to go back into the world to live their regular life, especially the "kings," those with the intention to do something with their new understanding. They wanted to learn in the monastery as fast as possible and then use what they learned to pursue their own ends. This is not necessarily an evil thing: every single wellness product, yoga modality, and medicine is created by some king who was given compassion by somebody like Sumedha Maharshi. Everybody has their own journey; Sumedha Maharshi understood that, and I understood it too. I also understood my own role in this, that I was there to help them out of their confusion.

Those merchants who came to the monastery, I could see how accelerated their spiritual growth was, how beautiful and complete their transformation. They connected to the Shambho, and the Sanjeevani of the universe flowed through them, healing them. They would sit in sadhana for hours upon hours in a state of complete bliss. But I would feel a little jealous because I was holding their hand and helping them reach their destination. Who was holding my hand and helping me reach my destination?

I had come to Lucknow to be healed, and on my path of healing, I had learned many things; I had helped many people. I had fulfilled the divine task of prati prasav, giving it to the seekers, no matter whether they were merchants or kings. I had done my job. But as I would see these merchants going into the deepest state, I wanted to experience that too. The thought of the shaktipat started to return to my mind: the taste my guru had given me, the bliss I had achieved and then lost.

I was like a pilot who flies his passengers to exotic locations where they will relax, find romance, be happy, but the pilot is stuck in the plane, forever helping others reach their destinations but never reaching his own. My inner Shiva was calling me, and as the desire grew, everything else started to seem like a distraction. I was like an addict going through withdrawal, where every event, every conversation, reminds them of that energy they yearn for. I would have little tastes of the shaktipat: when someone would go deep in the state of samadhi and their amrit would flow, and then a drop of what they were experiencing would fall on me. But those drops were not enough to quench my thirst.

This thought started as a small spark, and each day it continued to grow until it became a flame.

For thirty years, a very saintly monk lived inside a cave high on a mountain, doing mighty meditation and never speaking to another soul. As far as he was concerned, his meditations were helping him to be the best version of himself, and he didn't need to speak to anybody. Then one day, after all those years in the cave, he thought, "I've done it! I'm finally truly enlightened." So he left his cave on the mountain and went down to a small village in the foothills. A festival was underway, and the village was teeming with people crowding the streets. Just minutes after the monk entered the village, someone stepped on his toe.

"Ow!" the monk cried angrily. He turned to the person who had stepped on his toe and slapped him. "You blind idiot, can't you see what you just did?"

The other person saw that he had stepped on a monk's toe and was horrified. "I'm so sorry I hurt you!"

But the monk started running away.

"Wait, where are you going?" the other man called.

"I've just spent thirty years of my life in a cave, and I thought I was enlightened. I didn't even know there was this anger inside me until you stepped on my toe. Clearly, there's much work still to be done, so I'm going back to my cave."

You can sit in your cave for fifty years, sixty years, a hundred years, and you will think you're enlightened. But you won't know unless someone steps on your toe. Only then can you observe your reactions—otherwise, it's all an illusion.

If we do not connect with reality, we can be lost in fantasy. People would come to Rajasthan chasing a poetic ideal of spirituality. They would read an ancient text or spiritual book and gain these ideas about how the sky would open above them and a mystical portal would appear, or a dove would kiss their forehead. Illusion will never reap the spiritual rewards of a genuine connection that surpasses the fantasy.

The king who comes to the monastery and takes what it gives him then sells it for personal gain, that king I do not appreciate—but I understand. What made me sad was the kings who didn't even know what they were chasing. They have been told about a peacock, but now they are mistakenly looking for a crow. The two birds don't sound the same, and they don't look the same—so they will end up searching all their lives, never finding what they seek.

Through spending time with people, I gained two things. First, I could see the reality that transcended the poetry. I gained a much more grounded understanding of scripture based on real life. The second benefit I gained was a sense of self-awareness. When you see somebody else making a mistake, it frustrates you—then you realize that "oh, I do that same thing too."

But while I was appreciating and helping people and even growing, the question arose in me: *Who am I and why am I doing all this?* I felt that some key truth was eluding me, and there was a yearning within for something more.

These notions were spinning through my head all the time. They were like flies trapped in a room—buzzing and spinning and banging against the windows. According to Mashe, my Rudra granthi was closed: my head, my cognition. So these thoughts had nowhere to go, except to spin around and around in my head.

One day I was sitting with Tufan and Shambho. Shambho was frustrated because he had a bunch of gnats flying around his face, so he was swishing his tail to get rid of them. Tufan was agitated because he had a bunch of fleas he was trying to scratch away. And I was equally upset—but my fleas and gnats were internal, not external! I couldn't scratch them away; I couldn't flick them away with my tail. All three of us brothers, the dog, the bull, and me, were stuck in the same predicament.

Finally, one night, with great conviction, I called Babaji. Taking a deep breath, I told him, "My mind is not letting me do my work.

Everything is a distraction—there's this great desire, a longing, and I want to go on to the next step. Shiva is calling me. You are my guru; tell me what I must do."

My father could hear in my voice that I was like a pressure cooker, ready to explode.

"Ishan, first you must taste the amrit, the nectar of immortality."

The circle had become a whole: Suzie and Barbara had come to the monastery, looking for amrit. Now, I was to go out looking for amrit.

"What? Where do I find the amrit?" I asked my father.

"Son, you begin this life through the mother. Now you must begin your next life through the Mother."

He told me to go to Dakshineswar in Calcutta, to the temple of the Mother, Bhadrakali—one of the forms of the goddess Shakti.

"Do sadhana there, and the Mother will give you the path," Babaji said.

Never before had my guru been so direct in his instruction. I was ecstatic, overjoyed. I had never been to Calcutta, never traveled so far from the northern part of India where I had been born and raised.

That night, I packed my few belongings and went to the temple of Mahakaal to say my farewells there. From all the people I loved, I took their blessings. I bid farewell to Mahakaal and left with only a bag across my shoulder. As I walked out the door, I looked back just once. After that final glance, I set my sights on the path ahead.

Before me was uncertainty, behind me a weight that I had to let go. *Welcome to the spiritual path*, I said to myself.

And so my story as a student ended, and my story as a seeker began.

SAMADHI MEDITATION PRACTICE

Silently in your mind, chant the mantra *om*, repeating it over and over.

With each inhalation, chant *om*, and with each exhalation, chant *om*, keeping your breath slow and deep.

Do this for fifteen minutes.

PART FOUR

MASTERING THE SOUL
RETURN TO RAJASTHAN

CHAPTER 19
FACING THE DARK PASSENGER

जहाँ आस्था वहाँ रास्ता

Faith will find the way.

India is an ancient place. Over thousands of years, mighty kings have risen, and great empires have fallen. But why does an empire fall? There is a Sanskrit saying: "When the end is near, the brain starts working in reverse." In other words, even great kings will make foolish mistakes when destruction approaches.

As I started my travels across India, I thought about the great tales from the cultures of the East and the West. I thought of the Trojan War: Troy held back Agamemnon and his vast army for such a long time that Agamemnon had almost accepted defeat—until his commander in chief, Odysseus, devised the plan of the Trojan horse. They say the walls of Troy were built by the gods themselves, yet the Trojans opened the gate and allowed a wooden horse full of warriors in. What caused them to make such a mistake?

In the ancient Indian epic the Ramayana the hero Rama and

his brother Lakshmana were living in the forest. Lakshmana placed Rama's wife, Sita, within a boundary created with divine mantras. This magical barrier was impenetrable from the outside, so she would be safe from harm. However, the demon king Ravana came in disguise as a beggar. He approached Sita and said, "I am a hungry saint. Please give me some food." So Sita broke the boundary, came out, and gave food to Ravana. What made Sita fall for Ravana's trickery?

East and West alike, the mightiest warriors have a weak point. Achilles was unstoppable in battle, but all the Trojan prince Paris had to do was shoot him in the heel with an arrow, and Achilles died instantly. India had a great warrior, Duryodhana, whose weak spot was his thigh. All his opponent Bhima had to do was to strike his thigh with his mace, and the mighty Duryodhana was mortally wounded.

What is this weakness that the wise men of the past warned us about? What is this weakness that hides patiently inside, waiting for its time to strike like a rattlesnake in the grass? What is this thing that makes empires and heroes fall? And surely this element must still exist today, making us vulnerable to being tricked and led astray?

In my travels I passed by the relics of mighty empires, each one thousands of years old and bearing the legacy of men who, however briefly, could call themselves Great King.

At this time, I started to become aware of a noise—a disturbance—growing in my own mind.

You see, Rajasthan, Dwarka, and Lucknow were all consecrated lands. These lands where I grew up were like Shangri-la, where the eternal fountain of youth flowed. Anyone who came could bathe in the energy. People came with their stresses and sorrows, and they would be healed. I had lived within a divine boundary, but now I was outside that boundary.

There is a tale told of the sage Narada, who was meditating in a place blessed by Lord Shiva, where Shiva himself had also once meditated. In this place anyone who meditated was protected from the attachments, miseries, and illusions of the world. As Narada immersed himself in deep meditation there, some of the devas (celestial beings or gods) grew jealous of his spiritual achievements. To distract him from his path, they enlisted Kamadeva, the god of love and desire (similar to Cupid), to shoot his arrows of attraction at Narada. Their intention was to break Narada's concentration and dedication, making him fall prey to temporary desires and emotions.

Kamadeva shot his arrows, but because Narada sat in this consecrated space, not one arrow pierced him. Impressed by Narada's unwavering resolve, Kamadeva approached him and said, "You have achieved a level of divine excellence beyond even some of the gods. Only the most divine beings possess such power to resist temptation. You are truly great!"

Caught up in his meditation, Narada did not know why Kamadeva was praising him in this way. He started to think, *Am I really so extraordinary?* Filled with pride, he left the sacred land and went into the world to tell everyone about his greatness.

However, as soon as Narada crossed the boundary of the consecrated land, he was crushed by the very temptations and illusions he had previously been protected from. That weakness that makes heroes falter and empires fall took hold of Narada.

This story had been told to us boys in the monastery so we could understand the gift we had been bestowed with—and so we would understand that if we went beyond the boundary and we were not ready, there was something with the power to consume us. This Apasmara, or dark passenger, is the one responsible for the brain working in reverse, the one responsible for the fall of empires, the one who dances uncontrollably in the world we live in, causing chaos and corrupting the hearts and minds of all.

On some level, I had experience of this Apasmara in Dwarka when I went outside the boundary to the Western school. During the day, I would feel these dark emotions, but each night, when I returned to the ashram, the thoughts vanished, and I was free once again. Apasmara showed me his face, but he could not take control of me.

In Lucknow, too—after I broke my back, I passed many nights wondering, *How could I have made such a mistake?* But was it truly I thinking these thoughts, or the "I" who was weakened by the Apasmara—the Apasmara that whispers in your ear, quietly takes control over you, and pushes you into eternal sleep, making you live in a never-ending dream, stuck in a cycle of attachment, life, and death.

Now as I traveled outside the divine boundaries, the Apasmara started to show me his face once more.

One of the stories that captivated me in my childhood is of Bhasmasura, a classic case of someone corrupted by the Apasmara. Bhasmasura did a lot of meditation, prayer, and good deeds—all the practices that I had been taught. However, Bhasmasura wasn't connected to the infinite.

One day, Shiva came to Bhasmasura and said, "You have prayed so much. What do you want?"

"I want so much power that when I put my hand on someone's head, they become dust," he replied.

"Done," Shiva agreed.

"Yes!" Bhasmasura exulted. "I have this power; now I need to try it." He looked to the left. He saw nobody. He looked to the right. He saw nobody. Looking in front of him, he saw Shiva. "Aha, I'll try it on Shiva!"

Shiva ran for his life, and Bhasmasura chased him. Vishnu saw Shiva was in danger and thought, *I will save Shiva's life.*

Vishnu used his shape-shifting powers to take the form of a woman and called out to Bhasmasura, "Hey, what are you doing?"

"I want to try this new power I have to turn someone to dust," Bhasmasura replied.

The shape-shifter started laughing. "How can you be sure you have this power?"

"Oh, I did so much prayer, so much meditation that Shiva gave it to me."

"How do you know it was Shiva? It could have been a guy in a costume making a fool of you. I don't think you really have this power."

"I have the power!" Bhasmasura told him, becoming annoyed.

So the shape-shifter said, "Let's try it out. Put your hand on your head, and let's see what happens." Without thinking, Bhasmasura put his hand on his own head and—kaboom!—he was a pile of dust on the ground. His dark passenger made him so hungry for power, his brain worked in reverse and led to his destruction.

The monks in my tradition called the dark passenger our *samskara*, the subtle impressions of all our past actions; or our *sanchita karma*, the sum total of all our past deeds, both good and bad. It is a being that we have created, who lives inside us and wants to dominate us. Imagine that you are a robot. Who will control this robot?

There are two choices: the divine being that has been created by God itself; or the dark passenger, which you have created yourself through your traumas and pain and lifetimes of experiences that occurred before you were even born.

It begins for most of us as a whisper of doubt. When you walk out of your house, you wonder: *Should I take a left turn or a right?* Before, I wasn't even thinking of these things. Somebody told me, "Left turn!" And I would reply, "Sir, yes sir!" Now, I was on my own. If I took the left turn, the dark passenger started to feed me anxiety.

"What are you doing? You should have taken the right turn. Probably the treasure that you are seeking was over there."

Then the whisper becomes a voice, saying, "What are you doing? Where will you go? What is going to happen to you?" It creates an unknown that is full of doubt and fear.

At this time, the dark passenger wasn't strong enough to do very much because I had my spiritual practice, I had my trust, and I had my hope. Inside me were the two wolves, the good and the bad. I had been feeding the good wolf diligently with my practices, but unconsciously I had dropped crumbs for the bad wolf to feed on too. Now my wolves were preparing for the great confrontation that must inevitably happen.

Dakshineswar lies in Calcutta, which is probably the most chaotic city that you've ever seen. Yet amid such chaos there is beauty. Despite the apparent randomness, there is a structure. If we look through an electron microscope at a cell, it will seem that the atoms are in such flux. But in truth, that is what causes creation in the first place. I found the same in Calcutta.

I was transfixed and enamored with what I saw. All around me, the streets were teeming with locals and tourists, cars and auto-rickshaws, street vendors and stray dogs, but all of that fell away compared with the divine energy that reverberated everywhere.

All of my senses were awakened. Even the architecture was awe-inspiring: the Victoria Memorial, the Indian Museum, the Kalighat Kali Temple—each structure was gigantic, beautiful, you could say magnanimous. Even the chaos was magnanimous in its own way.

When you walk through Calcutta, you cannot help but be aware of the thousands of years of its history. This city has given birth to some of the greatest intellectuals, freedom fighters, and monks that India has ever seen. The two great monks that brought Eastern thought patterns to the West in this modern era, Swami Vivekananda and Paramahansa Yogananda, were both from Calcutta.

I was amazed. What could be in the waters or the rock beneath that makes this place so powerful?

Then I went to Dakshineswar, to the temple of the Mother Kali, and truly everything else fell away. In my tradition, Bhadrakali represents the great Mother of all the world, and she is most unique and beautiful to us Shiv Yogis. There are many forms of Shakti, and each person is attracted to a different one. For me, that attraction has always been to Bhadrakali. Many people are scared of this form of the Mother because she is ferocious. But to Shiv Yogis, there cannot be any form that is more beautiful. She is knowledge, she is power, she is prosperity, she is wisdom, she is everything.

Of all the places my father might have sent me, I was so fortunate that he sent me to the Mother. If it wasn't for her compassion and what she was about to show me, it would have taken me lifetimes to understand what this Apasmara was and how it influenced and controlled me.

When I arrived, the temple was about to close, but still there were a million people there. And when you are surrounded by a million people, there is no ego, no choice. All my martial arts skills were useless because when you are in the midst of a stampede, you go where the crowd takes you and you submit to the mercy of God.

The crowd swept me up from the outer gate, and in this multitude there was so much intimacy. I'd never been touched in so many places by so many people before. The sweat, the dirt, the grunting, the visceral nature of the stampede was incredible. But in the eyes of each person, there was a passion, a fire, a desire that some living in the West may never know.

And after a few minutes, or maybe a few hours—who knows? I did not have a watch back then—I was propelled into the temple complex. But when I reached it, I could not see the Mother through the crowds.

I was standing there, a bit sad, trying to catch my breath and thinking that I may as well just plunge back into the crowd outside. But then something happened. A thousand people moved their heads at once, at the perfect angle, so that I could see the face of Bhadrakali.

Her eyes were red. Her tongue was out. She held a sword coated with blood in one hand and a severed head in another.

When you look at a countenance like this, the dark passenger will fill you with disgust. But to the Shiva within me, she was the most beautiful, most divine thing I'd ever seen. I closed my eyes, and without thinking of life and limb, I sat down.

As I sat, consumed by the love, grace, and blessings of the Divine Mother, I asked her the question that was in my mind: *Why do men fail after every success? Why do empires fall? Why do saints topple?*

At that moment, the Mother smiled, and she became alive. She stopped all time, and she transported me to a different realm. I could feel her power and force, as if through her, the whole universe was communicating with me.

When I asked my question, the Mother guided me, gave me the knowledge, the divine vision, to know and see and understand the Apasmara. I did not know what I had done to deserve it, or if I was even worthy of it. But I was filled with delight.

The Mother showed me the dark passenger, the one who has led to the downfall of kings and saints; who has taken away the greatest gifts bestowed upon men; who has led to wars, corruption, and greed.

Even though I had been a monk all my life, now for the first time I could see the dark passenger because the Mother showed him to me. I felt at a loss. Not even the flood, not even my broken back—nothing had ever made me feel so lost. How could I overcome this dark passenger? I voiced my fears to the Mother.

"This fight is yours. Mahakaal and I will be with you," the Mother assured me.

"Mother, you, the creator of the world, can create universes in a second," I replied. "You, the destroyer of the world, can destroy universes in a second. Why can't you free me?"

And I heard her say, "Shiv Yog samadhi." This means "union with the divine in the state of samadhi." This is the state to which the greatest of the monks go when they become one with the Shiva themselves. It is something that I had barely experienced myself at the time of shaktipat. I did not know how I could do even more than I had done already.

The Mother knew my thoughts, and she smiled and said, "The *tap* must continue," referring to the intense meditative practices needed for spiritual growth.

"For how long?" I asked.

"Till nothing remains," she replied. "Till all that remains is the divine consciousness. Not even a dust particle, not even the clothes on your back, not even the flesh on your arms must remain. You will have to burn everything—because if you leave one thing, that is enough for the dark passenger to hide behind. So you must go."

"I'm tired," I told the Mother. "For so many years, almost two decades, I have done so much. How can I do more?"

She did not reply in words but showed me all the lifetimes I had lived. I saw the thousands of hours of prayers I had done, the thousands of sins I had committed. And I saw that in my past lifetimes, I had been a spiritual seeker, and I was not able to let go of the Rudra granthi: the blockage of the ego.

But because of what I was able to achieve in those lifetimes, the universe had blessed me with the tools that could help me in my journey. Because of the sadhana, the samadhi, the lifetimes I had spent on my quest, the Divine Mother blessed me with her vision.

Suddenly, it all made sense. Why I was given the life in the ashram. Why a divinity helped me fix my back. Why I was always helped in my meditations. Why I could experience this cosmic energy. I carried within myself a lifetime of divinity, and because of that, the universe took compassion on me. At my young age, it gave me the mantras and knowledge, the dedication and devotion of the ancients.

As the truth was revealed to me, I started to cry. In my tears, I felt a sense of hopelessness, surrender, and conviction. The hopelessness that if I could not achieve the ultimate goal in so many lifetimes, how would I be able to do it now? The surrender that said, "Mother, if you are blessing me, then please bless me in this too." And conviction, like a mother who anticipates and accepts the pain of labor, knowing that beyond childbirth is the greatest gift.

In that moment I was shaken, but through the Mother's grace in that divine place, I was unbroken and determined.

As the Mother blessed me, slowly my awareness started to change. I fell from that plane of consciousness, and I was transported back to the temple. The attendants were calling, "Time to go, time to go, time to go!"

I asked the Mother one last question.

"Mother, where do I go? What do I do?"

"Go to your Father. It is time. He's calling you home."

> ## SAMADHI
> ## MEDITATION PRACTICE
>
> Focus all your awareness on your brain and spinal cord.
>
> Silently repeat the mantra *om* in your mind. As you inhale with the mantra *om*, gently shift your awareness from the top of your head to the base of your spine. As you exhale with the mantra *om*, move your awareness from the coccyx through each vertebra to the top of your head. Inhale with your awareness moving from the head to the coccyx, and exhale with your awareness moving from the coccyx to the head. Let everything else fall away.
>
> Continue this process for fifteen minutes.

CHAPTER 20

GOING BACK TO THE BEGINNING

यो जागर्ति सुषुप्तिस्तो यस्य जरान्न विद्यते,
यस्य निर्वासनो बोधः स जीवन्मुक्त उच्यते।

The one who is awake even while in deep sleep, whose knowledge is free from past negative impressions, is said to be liberated.

I had read this statement in many scriptures; I had repeated it like a parrot in the various spiritual practices I had learned in my life. But for the first time, these words rose in me like an emotion I had never felt before. Realization burst into existence within me—a simple, natural acceptance, the way one accepts that the sun shines in the sky, the moon reflects the light of the sun, the waters of the ocean cover more than half the planet. On this day, through the grace of the Mother, I realized that I was immortal.

Bhadrakali had shown me many of my past lives, and in each of them I had come to understand the transient nature of the body. Yes, the body was born and the body died. But the *I*, the soul consciousness, the divinity within me, has always been immortal. And like the body wears clothes and removes them, so too the immortal self wears the body and lets it go.

In those past lives, however, I wasn't connected to the immortal self. I was connected to the body. When the body got sick, I felt that it was *I* who got sick. When the body died, each time the thought was there that *I* had died. The mind created attachment to transient things, and then the mind felt loss when the object of attachment was taken away.

In each of my past lives, I gained no understanding of the nature of the four shivlings: creation, maintenance, destruction, and evolution. And because there was no understanding, there was immense sorrow. Within me, I saw the Apasmara, the dark passenger, taking over my mind in each life. Like a puppet master, it slowly took away my realization of the immortal self, stripping from me the power and the wisdom of the immortal self and leaving only the attachment and the sorrow of the illusion that manifested in each life.

The Apasmara is a champion of creating attachment and sorrow, trials and tribulations, grief and misery. It slowly consumes one's life until, like any member of the animal kingdom, we are reduced to shelter and survival, producing offspring, escaping death and finally succumbing to it. In each life, when we do not connect to the real nature of the immortal self and remain burdened by illusion, the Apasmara claims its victory.

But in the last eight lives, something had started to change within me. The scriptures say that prayers to God, even if they are selfish in the beginning, will purify one's mind. As the devotion to God grows in intensity, eventually the devotee will desire nothing more than God. It is then that God shows grace by manifesting as a spiritual guide.

I had spent these past eight lifetimes mastering five skills:

Satsang: pursuing the company of great siddhas.

Shraddha: belief in the divine's existence, love, and grace.

Samarpan: the soul's surrender to the divine.

Sannyasa: complete renunciation of all transient things.

And finally, *samadhi*: in which we go deep within ourselves and merge with the divine consciousness.

Now, I knew that these five tools, these five *s*'s, would help lead me to the final *s*: *sakshatkar*—a state of self-realization and enlightenment, in which I would truly experience the divine.

Energy cannot be created nor destroyed. It is only converted from one form to another. For each action we do, there will be a reaction, a creation of energy. Because of the spiritual path that I had followed in my past lives, because of the blessing and love of Shiva and Shakti, the Father and the Mother, I was blessed that in this life, each of these skills I had learned would come back to me. In this life I was born in satsang, surrounded by divine men. In Lucknow and Dwarka I had learned shraddha, samarpan, and sannyasa: faith in the divine masters, surrender to their protocols, and setting aside worldly goals. Through shaktipat, I had learned to go deep into samadhi and access the divine power.

With these five skills, I was strong. But the Apasmara is as cunning as a fox. Just as my divine nature had created a core of divinity that cannot be destroyed, following me in this life and helping me in the spiritual journey, so too the manas putra, the negativity that I had created in the form of the Apasmara, had followed me, pushing me again toward illusion, toward maya.

As I sat, looking at my past lives that the Mother had revealed to me, I was filled with wonder at all the different paths to the supreme power I had walked on: sometimes through religion and spiritual practices, sometimes through devotion and perseverance. Dazed and delighted, I was filled with ecstasy as I contemplated the past. But as I relished my visions, that sly fox Apasmara started to whisper thoughts of the present in my ear.

It showed me visions of the world around me and what was happening in the name of religion. "Look how blessed you are, how lucky that the Mother loves you so much that she has shown you such wisdom. And now look at the world around you. In the name of religion, people push superstition, hatred, and resentment and draw others away from the divine. Doesn't that make you feel angry?"

How subtly the Apasmara sabotages our minds. My joy slipped away, and now I felt anger. I started to look around and think of all these people who do harm in the name of faith—who, instead of helping, push others away from their divine nature and into darkness. In my travels across India, I had seen this. Now, I became hyperaware of the misinterpretation of scriptures, the superstition peddled to create fear and paranoia. My anger grew.

Subconsciously, though, my divine traits had not left me. Like muscle memory for a martial artist after a long time away from their practice, I found my body going back to the satsang and the shraddha and the samarpan. I went to a Shiva temple, and I sat in contemplation.

Going Back to the Beginning

By now I had forgotten the wisdom that Bhadrakali had shown me: it was like a dream that drifts away with the morning light, and I had sunk deep into my dark emotions. As I sat there, a naga came over to me. Nagas are a type of saint who worship Shiva: they wear no clothes, they cover themselves in ashes, and their hair is matted into dreadlocks. Often they carry with them a weapon such as a cane or a spear.

The naga looked at me and said, "*Har Har.*"

I looked back at him and said in a voice devoid of feeling, "*Mahadev.*"

This is a form of chant, a call and response. It is like when somebody says, "Hello. How are you?" You say, "Fine. How are you?" Har Har Mahadev means "glory to Lord Shiva." Whenever someone says "Har Har," you reply, "Mahadev." You should say it with feeling, with devotion, with the heart.

"Har Har," the naga said again.

"Mahadev," I replied, but they were just words from my mouth, not from my soul.

The naga looked at me and started laughing. And he said, "You are so angry. Why?"

"Look around you," I said heatedly. "This holy culture, formed over thousands of years, its essence has been taken away, and petty superstition is all that is left. This is not even a flower, nor a picture of a flower—it is a hand pointing to a picture of a flower, and that is being presented as my people's knowledge."

The naga held a stick in his hand, and with it he touched my right elbow. I used to wear a heavy bracelet on my right wrist bearing the *sri yantra*, a symbol of devotion. The moment he touched my right elbow, the bracelet on my wrist, the necklace around my neck, and the rings on my fingers all fell off.

Now he had my attention.

"Ishan, let me tell you a story," he said.

"What story, Baba?" I replied. When you meet such people, you call them Baba as a mark of respect. "I'm angry. I'm ready to punch somebody. And you're saying you want to tell me a story?"

"I touched you with my stick once, and your jewelry fell off," the naga replied. "I'll touch you again, and you will be butt naked like me. Do you want that?"

"No, Baba. Tell me, tell me."

He told me a story from the Upanishads, the sacred texts of Hinduism.

Long ago, there were two monkeys and a sparrow. The two monkeys were out in the rain, while the sparrow was happily in its nest. One monkey told the other, "I have seen the humans make fire. And when they make fire, they can get warm, and they don't feel cold."

"How do we make fire?" the second monkey asked.

"We need a spark," his friend replied.

"How do we get a spark?"

"Look at all these fireflies," the first monkey suggested. "Let's catch one of them. They are sparks, so we can light a fire."

They caught one firefly and put it among some branches. Nothing happened. They took another firefly and put it in the wood. Again, nothing happened.

So the wise sparrow told the monkeys, "My dears, the firefly is not the right kind of spark. You have to go get the spark from the fire. The fire is different. The fire is hot. Let me explain to you how fire works."

The sparrow kept on talking and talking. "You can get fire from friction. You get friction when you take two stones and you rub them together—or you take a piece of wood and you rub it, and you get a spark."

The sparrow went on and on, until finally one monkey said, "Shut the hell up. Why can't you just shut up?"

He picked up the sparrow, threw it against the tree, and the sparrow died.

And the naga said to me, "Many monks have been led by the dark passenger to be the sparrow yelling among a crowd of monkeys. Do you want to be that sparrow?"

"No," I replied. "But why is all this happening? I want to do something."

"First, learn what to do," the naga told me. "Right now, you will tell people what *not* to do. But make your song so sweet that people set aside what they are doing just to listen to your song. It is not your place to tell people what is wrong. It is your place to sing, and the world will dance."

Then he started laughing and said, "Angry people don't sing very sweetly."

His laughter was so contagious, that even I started laughing with him.

The naga said to me, "Be aware. It is the Apasmara that distracts you. Once you have reached sakshatkar, once you have the wisdom and you have helped yourself, then you will have the power to help others if you choose. Until the time you reach that stage, everything is just a distraction."

Now I felt alert and aware, and I was surprised how easily my awareness had returned. Once again, the naga said, "Har Har."

With complete awareness in each cell of my body, I shouted, "Mahadev."

As I did, the memory of the truth given to me by the Divine Mother flashed in front of me, and my heart was filled with shraddha and samarpan. I understood: I had to be alert, constantly on my toes, aware of the Apasmara and everything that he said to me.

The naga had been kind. Shiva had come to bless me again in a different form. I looked at the naga and said, "Baba, the Mother has told me, 'Go to your Father.' What do I do? You have been so kind to me. Show me the path."

"Ishan, give me your hand," he replied. "Where you are going, you will need this."

The naga put something in my hand, and he said, "I'm hungry. Go get me food, and we can talk more."

I picked up my belongings, and I ran to get him food. I found a stall and bought some *aloo puri*: spiced potato curry with fried bread.

When I came back, the naga wasn't there. I looked everywhere. I asked a group of monks, "Where is the naga?"

"You saw him," one replied with a mischievous smile. "That is enough. Now get lost."

I opened my fist to see what the naga had given me. In my hand was a bundle of red cloth. When I unrolled the cloth, inside it was the parad shivling: made of mercury, this shivling signifies creation and realization.

I held on to the shivling, smiling. Suddenly, I recalled the one time I had really known the Father, the time I had been closest to divinity: in Rajasthan. I started to think about the first time my guru had shown me the parad shivling, the shivling of realization, evolution, sakshatkar.

The Mother had told me, "Go to the Father," and now I knew what she meant. She wanted me to go back to the beginning, to go back home.

This time I would return wiser, stronger, more aware of my divine traits. But that would come later. Right now, I had aloo puri in my hand that I needed to eat and enjoy.

> ## SAMADHI MEDITATION PRACTICE
>
> Visualize the crown chakra, at the top of your head, as a thousand-petaled lotus. Now imagine this lotus as the seat of the supreme being. Upon the seat, invoke, accept, and visualize the supreme being.
>
> As you inhale with the mantra *om*, feel God's light flowing from the top of your head down to the base of your spine. As you exhale with the mantra *om*, direct your consciousness from the base of your spine up to the god at the top of your head.
>
> Meditate on the idea that with each inhalation, you receive the divine light of your god, and with each exhalation, you raise your consciousness and surrender to the supreme being.

CHAPTER 21
YOGA IS FREEDOM IN ACTION

अज्ञानतिमिरान्धस्य ज्ञानाञ्जनशलाकया।
चक्षुरुन्मीलितं येन तस्मै श्रीगुरवे नमः।

Salutations to the guru who removes the darkness of ignorance from our inner eyes by applying the light of knowledge.

After the Mother had shown me my past, I felt like a person who has awakened from a dream. No matter how scary or beautiful a dream is, once you are awake it is very difficult to return to your dream. I felt, too, like a child who is sleeping blissfully in their bed and then is suddenly awakened by their loving mother because it is an important day and something urgent must be accomplished.

But what was the urgent task that I needed to accomplish now? What was the reason I needed to be awakened from my slumber?

Now, as I recalled my vision of the past, I saw my finite self, stuck in a room that was filling fast with water. In front of me was a gate, through which I must escape before I drowned. Beyond that gate lay the infinite self, the immortal self—my goal. But the gate was guarded by the illusionary self, which would not permit me to pass. It was the finite me, facing the illusionary self, barred from being one with the immortal self. The water would rise, and my finite self would drown. The game would reset and start again.

Thinking about that game and all the losses I had faced filled me with a sense of indifference toward everything around me. No flower's fragrance attracted me, no sweet bird's song, nor the colors of a butterfly, nor the sun's bright rays. I felt complete dispassion for this world and maybe even a bit of contempt for myself. For I had been through this circle so many times before, and now because I had awakened from the dream, I could not even go back. I had to live with this dispassion, this sadness. What started out as a very beautiful experience, a gift of divine energy from the Mother, slowly transformed into an awareness that I did not know what to do with it.

This dispassion was my companion as I traveled to the only place I had experienced the sense of safety that comes from a father. That place was where it all began: the ashram in Rajasthan, the land of Mahakaal and the holy siddhas. My roots.

Through my journey I was hungry, sleep deprived, and physically exhausted, yet I did not want to give any comfort to my body until these feelings had been resolved. Until I understood why after eight lifetimes of such intense spiritual desire, the ultimate goal had eluded me.

One day, as I trudged in my exhaustion, I felt the desert in the air at last. There was a dryness in it, the fragrance of sand. Then it was beneath my feet: the soft, soft sand. I had not walked on this sand for almost ten years. And now my feet were on it again, and so many memories of the past started flooding back. Even though my mind was still in a state of flux, my lips were smiling as I walked. I was back in Rajasthan, the landscape of my childhood.

That night when I was shaking with cold from the desert chill, in the distance I saw a fire. Nearer I walked, not even thinking where this solitary fire in the middle of nowhere had come from or who would light a fire in this desert landscape. I was drawn to the fire like a moth to the flame, and beneath a moonless sky with billions of stars, there was only the fire.

I sat on the warm sand by the fire and looked deep within its flame. Suddenly, this fire reminded me of the *yagya* fire sacrifices I did in Dwarka, and the fire around which we used to sit and tell stories in Rajasthan.

I gazed into the fire, and I said to myself, "I was their failure."

From the other side of the fire, a voice spoke. "There is no failure on the spiritual path. Even when we walk down a winding mountain pass in order to reach a higher peak, it is not a downfall. The only true setback is falling and not getting back up. If you continue, there is success."

It was a soft voice, a comforting voice, a divine voice.

"There is no bad fate or fall for one who has started on the path of goodness. The smallest good, the smallest dharma, helps one overcome great fears—and you, my child, have done a lot."

At the words *my child*, I looked up and saw that it was Babaji, the father of my body and my spiritual guide in this life. But he seemed different: young, like he used to be in Rajasthan. There was a glow around him: it could be the fire reflecting on his skin, but it looked like divinity. Whatever it was, I was happy to see him.

"Babaji, how come I have not reached the highest point after so many lifetimes?" I asked him.

"A person may spend a thousand lifetimes without the desire for awaking, without a yearning for yoga," he replied, meaning both the practices and the connection with the divine. "Such a person will be subjected to infinite birth and infinite death. Their growth will take lifetimes, and they will spend eternity being controlled by the Apasmara in a dream illusion state. Then something beautiful happens: through karma or a great blessing, a desire for yoga awakens in them. You are here because there is that desire within you."

I shook my head. "But Bhadrakali showed me I've had this intense desire for eight lifetimes, and each time there is the desire but not the completion."

Babaji chuckled. "A baby takes its own time learning how to walk. For a spiritual seeker, the distractions are greater, the pull toward maya—illusion—is stronger. Such a person may start spiritual practices but become lazy and distracted. They may be attracted toward satsang, sadhana, even sannyasa. But such desires are like trying to light a candle in the wind. Sooner or later, the flame flickers out. But even if the flame exists for a short time, slowly the illusions start to dissolve."

He gestured at me. "In your past eight lifetimes, you found yourself born in the house of the rich. Among such comfort, sometimes you got distracted and yoga was not achieved. But because the desire remained, you were born in the house of the pious, so you grew a little more. Now, when you are almost ready, you are born in the house of seekers, the lineage of wise yogis. Understand how rare and fortunate your birth is, that you are blessed with such divine spiritual practices at an early age, under proper guidance."

I recalled what I had learned many years before: every child is born a rock, and if they are lucky, they meet siddhas who see the beauty within. They spend the time to carve the child, shape them, give them purpose. It was my good fortune to be such a rock.

Babaji saw the understanding lighting my face. "You are blessed with the divinity that can help you wake up and witness the illusionary self, the Apasmara, that has hindered your growth."

"I see the Apasmara, but I still don't understand how it has such power over me," I said.

My guru smiled. "It controls you by playing with your mind. It uses fear and desire together to control you. It takes over your imagination, and the fear arises that you are incomplete—that you, the infinite immortal being, are not good enough. Then you are possessed by the notion that if you possess this thing or that thing, you will be complete. It makes you run after things, again and again.

"Imagine if the shining sun in the sky said, 'I will be complete only if I have a fancy car.' Or if the mighty flowing river said, 'I will be complete only if the king's ship sails upon me.' The Apasmara affects the mind by causing it to brood over things, always suggesting new forms of enjoyment and distraction to please the senses. It affects the memory by telling you to repeat a certain experience or improve that experience. Into your head it puts a little fear, some insecurity, some doubt, and says, 'If only you accomplished this or achieved that, you would be free.' It affects the imagination by creating images in which you are free, but the image keeps changing the more you accomplish, the goal further away than when you started. The Apasmara fills you with longing when you look at others, making you devalue what you have and overvalue what others have. And all the time, getting further away from the goal of yoga, the divine self."

As I sat there listening to my guru, I felt another presence. Through the fire I could see the dark passenger, the Apasmara, looking at me, waiting for the fire to die down so that it could try to seduce me one more time with another transient desire, another illusion of achievement. Beneath the starry sky, sitting on the desert sand beside the fire that was slowly dying down, I was with the guru giving me wisdom and the Apasmara waiting for the guru to stop.

Gazing at the flames, I tried to calculate how long the fire might last. "How may I free myself once and for all?" I asked my guru.

He smiled, as if amused by my innocence. "Son, there is no such thing as forever on this planet Earth. While you dwell in this dimension, you must follow its rules. But there are some things that can help you. Try to meditate and drop your identification with the finite self, because it is the finite self that is creating these thoughts that you are incomplete, you will die, you will drown. As you drop the identification with the finite, you will start to walk toward awareness."

"How can I do that, Babaji?"

"Bring your intention and awareness inward," he replied. "Understand that all desire for external gratification is false. It is the Apasmara making you think that happiness will occur when you get certain objects in life. The presence or absence of an object does not create happiness. It is our mind and our thoughts alone that have the power to create happiness. When we are full, even the mind can make us hungry. Go to the state of no mind—only then will there be complete freedom."

The flames flickered in a faint breeze across the desert sand. Babaji continued.

"You are blessed, son, because through the grace of the Mother you have developed a dispassion. Such indifference is the greatest gift because it allows you to go toward yoga. People mistake this dispassion for sadness; they think they have a mental health issue, some kind of depression, and they try to cure it without understanding its root cause.

Yoga Is Freedom in Action

But such dispassion releases you from the external world and allows you to commence an inner journey. It is this state you have wanted for such a long time. There are many in the world who want to enter this state of no mind, in which there is freedom from the Apasmara. They try to reach it through substances, ultimately leading to addiction. Yet when the effect of the substance wears away, the Apasmara shows its face again."

My guru leaned forward a little, emphasizing his words. "Son, you must go to the state of no mind, through the door, beyond which lies the infinite self. When you are in this place, you do not hear, see, or know anything else, and this is the infinite. And only in this infinity is there happiness. In this beautiful state, son, lies your bliss. "

I heard my guru's words. I saw the Apasmara, still a shadow beyond the fire. Gradually, the flames started to die. As the last flames flickered out, a thought came to me. How good it would be if I could only sit here, free from all desires, and just listen to Babaji. I would be melted by his words and forget the Apasmara. How beautiful it would be if Babaji's words would give me the freedom I yearned for, like once he had given the shaktipat. Even as the thought crossed my mind, my guru's voice resonated powerfully through me.

"Son, yoga is not freedom *from* action. It is freedom *in* action. To be a realized soul, to be one with the infinite, you must act while being in a state of freedom."

Freedom was the last word I heard. As the fire became embers and the embers turned to ash, I felt weary. Meditating on the divine words I had heard, I fell asleep.

I woke with the sun shining on my face, and I looked at the pile of ash in front of me. Beyond the ash I could see an impression in the sand, as if someone had sat with me through the night. But I was alone once again. I knew my guru had been here but in which form—mortal or immortal? Was I back at the Rajasthan ashram?

Gazing all around me, I noticed that although there was an impression from someone sitting on the sand, there were no footprints. And now I could see I was in a cremation ground, where people come to burn the bodies of their loved ones. Behind me were the ashes from recent funeral pyres, and around them the ashes of countless pyres burned through many years. As I gazed at the ashes, I felt as if through the grace of the guru and the sadhana, the samadhi and the shraddha, these funeral pyres were the pyres of my own past lives, the ashes of my own desires that were created by the Apasmara.

Directly before me was the funeral pyre of any fear and doubt that I may have had, for my guru had given me the divine wisdom. I must go inside. My Mother had sent me to the Father, and the Father had showed me the path. He had come in a divine form, and he had guided me toward the light, toward the state of no mind, toward freedom from the Apasmara.

The funeral pyre was not for the Apasmara; it was a force of nature, and it did what was its nature to do. The funeral pyre was for my finite self. The Apasmara had control only while the finite remained. When the finite is gone, there cannot be any shadow. I thought of a three-bladed fan. When the fan is not moving you can see the blades and their shadows. But when the fan spins very fast, there are no blades, no shadows. Freedom in action—I had to raise my own consciousness.

I knew where I was, and I was ready to walk through the sun toward the temple of Mahadev in Rajasthan, where I was born. For the walk was not a physical journey. From the funeral pyre to Shiva, it was an internal walk, leading me through the state of no mind to the immortal self.

After so long I could taste it, and I was so happy. Still I sensed the Apasmara walking with me, and even though I ignored the thoughts and desires it created, it didn't give up or leave my side.

I didn't care. Let him do what he wanted. I had my own destiny.

> ## SAMADHI
> ## MEDITATION PRACTICE
>
> Sit comfortably, relax, and close your eyes.
>
> Bring your awareness to a point where your entire life is behind you, and all that lies ahead is a gate—the gate of death. As you face this gate, observe and accept any thoughts that arise. Witness the emotions and unresolved issues you wish to release before passing through the gate. Reflect on the most important aspects of your life that you are leaving behind.
>
> For today, allow death to be your teacher, guiding you in understanding what truly matters and what you need to let go of.
>
> Meditate on this feeling as long as you can.

CHAPTER 22
JOINING THE DANCE OF IMMORTALITY

मात्रास्वप्रत्ययसंधाने नष्टस्य पुनरुत्थानम् शिवतुल्यो जायते ।

On believing firmly that everything is one with one's own self, the highest state of consciousness that had disappeared rises again. One becomes equal to Shiva.

They say it is impossible to find the light without the guidance of the guru.

I took the guru's blessings, and after almost eleven years, I once again entered the sacred grounds of the Rajasthan ashram.

The landscape there had changed. Where once was a bustling, thriving community, now all I could see was sand—and amid it, a path that led to the temple of Mahadev. The structure looked smaller than I remembered; maybe I had just become bigger.

But the mountains were as they always had been. I could still see the path that the caravans of goat herders used to take, the same path they had been following for thousands of years.

When I reached the temple, I fell on my knees, and suddenly,

I was filled with acceptance that good things would happen. There is a difference between acceptance and imagination. If I tell you to imagine a dragon, you'll see it in your mind; maybe you will envisage a Norse dragon or a Chinese dragon. But if you're sitting in a dark room, and I tell you to take your awareness to the sun, you do not need to imagine. You know it's outside; all you have to do is come out of the room and the sun is there. Acceptance comes from a sense of awareness, and that acceptance and awareness bring hope and faith. It is that faith that gives you the power of perseverance.

Finally, I was at the land of the Father as the Divine Mother had guided me. At last, I didn't *think* that I would succeed in reaching my goal—I *knew*. Too many blessings had been given to me, too much guidance, for me to waste them. I had to seize the moment.

Through the guidance I had been given and the past lives I've seen, I knew that so many times opportunity comes, divinity comes, and people are too busy, too lazy. Consumed by transient distractions, fleeting stressors, and superfluous concerns, we forget what is important. Now, I knew what was of real value, and I had to respect the gifts I had created. Because just as I was aware of my divinity, I was also aware of the Apasmara sneaking behind me, my own creation. They say that you shall reap what you sow, and over time, over millennia, all the times I did not forgive, all the times I let hate conquer my heart, all the times I chose anger over forgiveness, I strengthened the Apasmara. I created its nature, which inclined toward the negative, and now it walked with me. But the Apasmara was as confused as I that it was following me, because it reasoned, "Ishan created me, so he should follow me."

Every villain thinks they are the hero of their own story. I'm sure the Apasmara thought it was trying to help me. When I looked at the Apasmara, I could see it wasn't acting from malice; it was simply following its nature.

Seeing this, every time the Apasmara sneaked a hateful thought into my mind, every time it attracted me to an object that wasn't my goal, I could not hate it.

I entered the temple, and in front of me lay all the forms of Shiva: the creator, the sustainer, the destroyer; the jyotirlinga, the infinite, the divine energy. It was then that I felt I had finally reached the point that my guru had made me meditate on, long ago in Rajasthan. "Take your awareness to the point at the end of life, when there is nothing in front of you except a door. That door is death. All life, all purpose, all choices are behind you, and you must walk through. When you pass through that door, the immortal self will be revealed to you."

I had taken all the learning and divinity that had been given to me, and I was as strong as I could be. Did I have a fear somewhere in my heart that I could be stronger or wiser, that I could have meditated more? Yes, the fear was there. I had been told I was not like my guru or the other monks, after all. But I had no time to focus on the fear. I remembered the lessons of the mantras from Dwarka, of perseverance from Lucknow, and I started.

I began with the mantras of invocation. From there, I started the breathwork, the prelude to the prati prasav. As I started the prati prasav, I could now see my thoughts and memories, but not in a way that they affected me; I just witnessed them. No matter what thought came, I had no judgment toward it.

"This is it!" I thought. "I've reached my goal. I have won."

Just before we receive the amrit, that is when the vish comes. I was ascending higher and higher into the state of samadhi, but in that moment the Apasmara appeared in front of me. When I looked at the Apasmara, I saw within it all my bad thoughts, bad choices, bad karmas—not just of this life, but all my lives combined. I was an ant looking at the Himalayas, and I had to spend an eternity (which I did not have as the finite self!) taking the mountain apart rock by rock, sand particle by sand particle.

For a moment, I gave up. But then the lessons of Lucknow rose up in me. I must persevere; I must continue my sadhana. In my heart a voice spoke: *There is no greater energy than the god from whom I have come and the god to whom I will return.* So I started to create the divine fire, and I projected that fire toward the Apasmara, thinking that if I destroyed it, I would win. But no matter what I did, I grew weaker while the Apasmara grew stronger.

For hours, days, nights, I used every mantra that I had, every sadhana I could remember, every breathwork I was capable of. I remained in that temple, and from the outside, it must have looked like a madman was sitting in there. But I remembered that my guru had told me, "Those who do not complete the path of yoga go back to the same cycle of life and death." This was it; this was my chance. If I did not accomplish it in this lifetime, then I did not know in which lifetime I would do it; I only knew I could not stay as the finite self.

And so I continued. I wanted to destroy the Apasmara, but finally I was exhausted. Physically, mentally, emotionally, I had nothing left. With the last ounce of energy that remained in me, I held on to the shivling—the divine, Mahakaal. And I created one last thought in my mind: *I surrender.*

Sometimes that's all we have: faith. We can do whatever we are capable of, but success lies in the hands of Mahakaal.

I surrender.

With that thought, another came: *Shiv, Shivanand, Shiv Yogi.*

I remembered my guru's words: "Son, you must go to the state of no mind, through the door beyond which lies the infinite itself, the place in which you will not hear, see, or know anything. That is where bliss lies."

As the emotion of surrender rose in me, I started to think that I was the *seer*, experiencing everything around me, while the *seen* was the experience, the nonself. The apparent existence of the duality of seer and seen creates the possibility of bondage, by which I mean the illusions and attachments my guru had shown me. But what if there is no duality? Then who could get bound by whom?

It occurred to me that if I could reach the place where there exists no notion of the other; no I, me, mine; no superiority and inferiority; no like and dislike; no Apasmar, no foe; no desire, greed, or anger—maybe then I could let go of all the conflicts and sorrows that are created by duality. At that moment I felt that Mahakaal was ready to be one with me, the Apasmar was stopping me, and I was putting in such a mighty effort to overcome it. What if there is no duality? What if in this moment of surrender, I let go?

Looking at Mahakaal, I remembered all the times I would pray and give offerings to Mahadev: flowers from the tree, fruits from the orchard, things that were never mine. Today, rather than offering up flowers and fruit, I would let go of my illusions and attachment. One by one, thoughts of *me, mine, I* started to come. Just as the tree drops each leaf, I started to drop each thought before Mahadev, saying to myself: *It all comes from the world, and the world comes from you. There is no me, there is no mine. It all is you. You are the ocean, and all of creation is just the waves that come from you. Today, let it go back to you. All thoughts of conquest, resentment, even fear of the Apasmar.*

I surrendered to Mahadev. Slowly, I let go of all concepts of the inner and outer world until just the *I* remained. This *I* was the pure self that was there before every experience, during every experience, and will exist even after every experience. The world and its attachments now felt unreal, and this *I* alone remained.

Finally, when it was only the *I* and Mahadev, I let go. How could there be an *I* when each ray of light is an extension of the sun, when each drop of water is an extension of the ocean, when all creation is a projection of the supreme consciousness? So I surrendered the self, the last ounce of ego. I surrendered the *I* to Shiva.

In that moment, I felt the divinity of Mahadev flow toward me like a blinding light, through the top of my head as if the infinite universe burst into me, shattering the Rudra granthi. I did not know if the light was entering me, or if I was rising into the light. The thought, *I surrender to Shiva* became *I am Shiva*.

No longer was there any duality. No yogi worshiping Mahadev, trying to overcome the Apasmar. It was just Shiva, through whom all creation manifests and to whom all creation returns. Only the light existed, and I did not hear, see, or know anything else. As I experienced this light and this divinity, the Shakti took me deep, deep into a place of infinity. It was a place I had visited before, the place my guru's shaktipat had taken me, where I had felt one with infinity. I was one with the immortal self.

In that state, I felt oneness with my guru. I could touch, feel, taste, smell everything he had experienced; I could think every thought he had conceived in every moment he had lived. All the gurus who had walked before me, I could live their lifetimes in an instant.

In this oneness, I felt free. I laughed because all my life I had thought I was free because I could think and say whatever I wanted to and walk wherever I chose. But that wasn't freedom. For lifetimes, I had been in a state of bondage, bound by sorrow, fear, and helplessness. Finally, I understood the nature of my captivity, and I was grateful for the liberation I now felt. I am the universe, and the universe is one with me. My journey through many lifetimes was complete. I was free. I was immortal.

In that state of completion, I had a choice. Should I remain in this divine space, or should I go back to the Earth to live my life? If I stayed, I would be complete, happy. But if I returned, I could give back to my spiritual family that had given me so much, and I could help those who need guidance, just like I was helped by the Siddhas. If I went back to the Earth, it is the nature of the third dimension to create duality, negativity, and attachment. For even Shiva in that dimension could create the Andhakasura.

I took a deep breath, one with Shiva. Through the grace of Shiva, through the oneness with Shiva, I was at a stage beyond dos and don'ts.

I remembered that even realized beings must fulfill their dharma, their duty. The thought came to me: *I will walk the Earth.*

As my infinite self still, the whole universe before me took the form of Nataraj: Lord Shiva as the dancer, powerful, strong, divine, performing the dance of creation, manifestation, and destruction. Beneath his feet was the Apasmara, immobile and powerless. Two immortals, fated to be together in an eternal dance. All divine goals were achieved with the Apasmara controlled under Shiva's foot. And I knew the path of the Shiv Yogi.

I returned to planet Earth. My body was as strong as it had been in Lucknow, before my journey began, without an ounce of weakness or fatigue. Even though I had not eaten for who knows how long, I felt stronger than any superhero.

If ever this body, this life, this mind created the manas putra, I knew it was the Apasmara's nature to create duality between me and Mahadev, to make me attach to the transient body, to make me feel anger. I knew the Apasmara would fill my heart with rage, locking me into an eternity of war and misery. But I also knew it was not in my nature to engage the Apasmara, but like Shiva as Nataraj, I could control it beneath my feet: through my meditation, my practice, my sadhanas, and my samadhi.

Through the grace of Shiva, I walked out of that temple an enlightened being, one with the immortal self. In the distance I saw the mango grove as I saw it when I was a child. A single tree was laden with mangoes shining in the sun like the finest Sri Lankan yellow sapphires. I went to pluck a mango, making a pile of the juiciest ones, ready to eat. Suddenly, I heard the sound of monkeys jumping down from the tree to take mangoes from the pile I had made. My mind created a thought: *I'll pick up that stick and chase away the monkeys. These are my mangoes!*

And with that thought, I smiled. The Apasmara had started again. But like Nataraj, I focused on my breath, chanted the mantra, became strong, and put the Apasmara beneath my feet. "There are plenty of mangoes, enough to share with the monkeys."

"*Share*? You want to share the mangoes with the monkeys?" The Apasmara's voice was crafty.

"Not just with the monkeys," I replied, "with the whole world. My dear Apasmara, Shiva will control you. Shiva will shine."

I felt accomplished and divine. As I went to take my share of the mangoes, I remembered the time I had spent with Suzie and Barbara. I had dreamed of being Hanuman and taking Sanjeevani to the world, and it seemed to me that now it was time to fulfill that dream.

"I will be with you, waiting for a chance to slip out," the Apasmara whispered slyly.

Like the cosmic Shiva, I just smiled and said, "Let's dance."

SAMADHI MEDITATION PRACTICE

From within your crown chakra, visualize and embrace the presence of your god, cultivating a deep sense of love and gratitude toward the supreme being.

Inhale with the mantra *om*, feeling God's light flowing from the crown of your head throughout your entire body.

As you exhale with the mantra *om*, sense your consciousness rising up from each cell, merging with the supreme being at the crown. As you inhale, experience a sense of rebirth; as you exhale, let go of the body.

Meditate on your oneness with the supreme being. Meditate on the thought: *I am one with infinite. I am one with my immortal self. I am Shiva.*

Continue this practice for twenty minutes. Do this every evening before you sleep.

YOUR IMMORTAL SELF

Here at the end, we come back to the two birds perched in a tree. When you started reading this book, your mind was connected to the lower bird, which was loud and agitated, hopping from one branch to another. Your mind was asleep, unknowingly attached to everything finite around you. As your consciousness has risen, you have connected to the higher bird, your wise subconscious, and real knowledge has entered into your seeker's mind. This is the awareness of your immortal being.

Now you know that you have the means to enter into a state where your consciousness rises—the state of samadhi. Any person can enter this state of divinity and access the profound wisdom that lies dormant within them. After all, I was very young when I experienced the events I have shown you in this book. I was just twelve years old when I left Rajasthan, then I was in Dwarka for five years and Lucknow for three, before spending three months crossing India in my travels. In Western terms I was barely into adulthood when I found enlightenment. So you see, these practices can bring us to immortality at any age.

To reach this state, guidance is sometimes necessary, and this book can act like the guidance of the holy siddhas. If you are attentive to the teachings in this book, they will create a new frame: the desire for higher knowledge. Through the continuous practice of meditation, this knowledge will slowly unfold within you.

In the final chapters of this book, the Father pushes me to the Mother, then the Mother pushes me to the Father. It is a beautiful metaphor for meditation, because in the Eastern meditative sciences the crown is the seat of Shiva, and the base of the spine is the seat of Shakti. In between the crown and the coccyx, between Shiva and Shakti, lies the whole universe. That is why they say the universe is within me: I am created from the universe, and I have the universe within me. That is why if I understand myself, then I understand the universe. The meditation I have given you in the final chapter, when we move from Shiva to Shakti, and then from Shakti to Shiva, allows a seeker to know themselves, go deep in themselves to raise their consciousness, letting go of the deceptions of the mind and becoming one with the immortal self.

The meditation practices I have shown you can be the beginning of a beautiful journey to find a new strength, enabling you to push through any turmoil life has put you through. Most importantly, as you strengthen in the state of samadhi, you will have the power to overcome the Apasmara. Your dark passenger may feel invincible, but in your story, the real power is not the Apasmara. It is you. It has always been you, and as you connect to that understanding, you will find that every single day you have the power to overcome, to persevere, to be resilient.

If, through this book, you can tap even a fraction of that power, that will be enough to overcome any Apasmara that you may have dancing around you.

I hope this book and the practices and the knowledge it contains somehow motivate you and help you in your life's journey.

GLOSSARY

abhinivesh: Clinging to bodily life because of fear of death.
Adinath: "The first lord," often referring to Lord Shiva in Hinduism.
advaita: "Nonduality," a concept in Hindu philosophy that emphasizes the oneness of all existence.
amrit: "Nectar of immortality."
amrit manthan: "Churning of the ocean"; in Hindu mythology, symbolizing the quest for immortality.
Andhakasura: A demon in Hindu mythology known for his blindness and intense darkness, symbolizing ignorance and evil.
antim yatra: The final journey or last rites performed for a deceased person in Hindu tradition. It involves rituals and ceremonies to honor the departed soul and ensure its safe passage to the afterlife.
anusthan sankalp: A resolution to perform a specific spiritual ritual with dedication and discipline. It involves making a commitment to undertake certain practices or observances to achieve a particular goal.
Apasmara: A demon in Hindu mythology symbolizing ignorance and forgetfulness; he represents the affliction of spiritual ignorance.

Glossary

Arjuna: One of the five Pandava brothers, who are the heroes of the Indian epic the Mahabharata. Arjuna, son of the god Indra, is renowned for his prowess in archery and his dedication to righteousness.

arti: A significant ritual in Hindu worship that involves the presentation of a lighted lamp or candle (often called a *diya*) along with the recitation of hymns before a deity's image. The light symbolizes divine presence and is meant to dispel darkness and ignorance.

asana: In yoga, a posture or pose practiced to maintain physical health, flexibility, and mental balance.

asmita: "Ego" or "sense of I-ness," often leading to a sense of individuality and pride. In spiritual contexts, asmita is viewed as an obstacle to achieving self-realization and spiritual liberation.

asura: In Hindu mythology, a class of powerful, often malevolent beings or demons. They are typically opposed to the devas (gods) and are associated with chaos, darkness, and material desires.

avidya: "Ignorance" or "lack of knowledge"; the ignorance of one's true nature and the ultimate reality, which is considered the root cause of suffering and the cycle of birth and rebirth (samsara).

bandha: "Bond" or "binding"; in yoga and spiritual contexts, it refers to specific bodily locks or energy seals used to control the flow of prana and enhance the effectiveness of asanas and meditation.

Bhadrakali: A fierce and protective form of the goddess Kali in Hinduism. Often depicted as a powerful deity who embodies both auspiciousness and formidable strength, Bhadrakali is worshipped for her protective qualities, as well as her ability to remove obstacles and grant blessings.

Bhagavad Gita: The 700-verse Hindu scripture that is part of the Indian epic Mahabharata. A key work in Hindu philosophy, it features a dialogue between Prince Arjuna and the god Krishna, exploring paths to spiritual realization, including devotion, knowledge, and action.

Bhasmasura: A demon who received a boon from Lord Shiva to turn anyone into ashes by touch.

bija: "Seed"; in Hinduism and Buddhism, it often refers to a symbolic seed or essence from which something grows or develops. It is commonly used in mantras (seed syllables) and represents the fundamental sound or vibration in spiritual practices.

Brahma muhurta: A period of time in the early morning, approximately one and a half hours before sunrise, considered highly auspicious in Hinduism.

chakra: An energy center in the body; there are seven aligned along the spine, each governing different physical, emotional, and spiritual aspects.

dharma: The moral and ethical duties and responsibilities based on one's role in life. It also refers to the Buddha's teachings for enlightenment. In the cosmic order, it refers to the natural order and laws governing the universe, ensuring balance and harmony.

dvesha: "Hatred" or "aversion"; it refers to intense dislike or animosity toward someone or something.

Gorakhnath: An early eleventh-century Hindu yogi, mahasiddha, and saint who was the founder of the Nath Hindu monastic movement in India. His followers are popularly known as jogis or shivyogis. He comes from Shiv Yog lineage, and is known for his profound influence on yoga and mysticism.

granthi: An energy knot or blockage in the subtle body (beyond the physical, mental, and spiritual), according to Indian yogic and spiritual traditions. The three main granthis are: Brahma granthi, linked to material attachment; Vishnu granthi, linked to emotional attachment; and Rudra granthi, linked to spiritual ego. Clearing these knots is essential for spiritual progress.

halahal vish: The deadly poison that emerged during amrit manthan (churning of the ocean) in Hindu mythology.

Hanuman: A revered deity in Hinduism and a central figure in the epic Ramayana, known for his ability to fly, his incredible feats, and his role in the rescue of Sita, Rama's wife, from the demon king Ravana.

Har Har Mahadev: A powerful chant in Hinduism, particularly in the worship of Lord Shiva. It's commonly used in temples, religious ceremonies, and festivals to invoke Shiva's blessings.

jup: Also spelled *jap*, this is a spiritual practice involving the repetitive chanting or recitation of a mantra. Jup can be silent, whispered, or chanted aloud.

jyotirlinga: The term combines two Sanskrit words: *jyoti*, meaning "light or radiance," and *linga*, which is a symbolic representation of Shiva. A jyotirlinga is believed to be a self-manifested form of Shiva, where the deity appeared as a column of light. Unlike regular Shiva lingas, which are typically installed and worshipped by devotees, jyotirlingas are considered naturally occurring. There are twelve jyotirlingas in India with different names and wonderful history.

Kalari: Also known as Kalaripayattu, an ancient martial art form that originated in the southern Indian state of Kerala; it combines physical training with mental discipline, spirituality, and self-defense techniques. It also incorporates yoga-like movements, meditation, and breathing exercises.

Kamadeva: The Hindu god of love and desire. His wife is Rati, the goddess of pleasure.

Glossary

karma: "Action" or "deed"; karma refers to the principle of cause and effect where a person's actions (good or bad) influence their future experiences through the cycle of birth, death, and rebirth (samsara).

Krishna: A major Hindu deity, considered the eighth avatar of Vishnu, Krishna is known for his roles as a divine lover, heroic prince, and wise teacher. He is often depicted playing a flute and is revered for his wisdom and divine playfulness.

kundalini shakti: A form of divine feminine energy believed to reside at the base of the spine in the root chakra. When awakened through spiritual practices, it rises through the chakras, leading to spiritual enlightenment and self-realization.

Mabhadrakali: A divine form of Maa Adhya Shakti, the Supreme Mother.

madhyama: "Middle"; it also refers to four levels of speech: vaikhari, when you use your voice to tell what you're thinking; madhyama, the thoughts in your head before you say them out loud; pashyanti, imagining a picture in your mind but not talking about it yet; and para, the very beginning of a thought, where it's just a feeling.

Mahadev: The supreme lord, Shiva.

Mahakaal: A form of Lord Shiva, meaning "Great Time" or "Lord of Time." He represents the power over time and death, symbolizing destruction and regeneration.

mahasiddha: "Great accomplished one"; denotes someone who has achieved high levels of spiritual realization and mastery over esoteric practices. It refers to a highly accomplished and enlightened being in various Indian spiritual traditions.

manas putra: "Child born of the mind"; refers to entities created through mental concentration or thought.

mantra: A sacred word, sound, or phrase in Hinduism, Buddhism, and other spiritual practices, repeated during meditation or prayer. The repetition of mantras is believed to focus the mind, invoke spiritual power, and aid in achieving specific spiritual goals.

maya: "Illusion"; maya represents the deceptive nature of the material world, which masks the true, unchanging reality.

meypayattu: The physical training aspect of Kalari training, imparting strength to the body and the mind.

moh: "Attachment" or "infatuation."

nadi: Energy channel in the body, according to yoga and Ayurveda, that carries vital energy (prana). Balancing the nadis is key in practices like pranayama and meditation.

namaste: A deeply rooted traditional greeting in India that translates to "I bow to you" or "I honor the divine in you."

Narada: A prominent sage in Hinduism, known for his role as a divine messenger and devotee of Lord Vishnu.

Narayana: "Refuge of all beings" or "shelter of mankind"; Narayana, as Vishnu, is regarded as the preserver and protector of the universe, responsible for maintaining cosmic order and harmony.

narmadeshwar shivling: A sacred Shiva lingam made from river stone found in the Narmada River, revered for its purity and spiritual significance. It is used in worship to symbolize Lord Shiva's formless divine nature.

Nataraj: The depiction of Lord Shiva as the cosmic dancer, symbolizing the universe's cycles of creation, preservation, and destruction.

Nilakanta: An epithet of Lord Shiva, meaning "Blue-throated One," referring to his act of drinking poison, which turned his throat blue during the churning of the ocean. It highlights Shiva's protective and sacrificial nature.

Glossary

Paramahansa Yogananda: Born in 1893, Yogananda is known as "the Father of yoga in the West." He introduced millions to meditation and Kriya yoga, and his book *Autobiography of a Yogi* has sold over four million copies.

parad shivling: A sacred Shiva lingam made from mercury, revered for its spiritual significance and believed to enhance divine energy and healing.

parampara: A traditional lineage or succession in Hinduism, signifying the transmission of knowledge and practices from teacher to disciple across generations.

paravani: The highest, divine sound or the ultimate expression of truth. It refers to the ultimate divine sound representing the primordial vibration underlying all creation.

pashyanti: One of the four levels of speech, pashyanti refers to imagining a picture in your mind but not talking about it yet. Pashyanti is linked to deeper, intuitive understanding and spiritual insight.

prana: "Life force" or "vital energy."

pranayama: A practice in yoga involving the control and regulation of breath, essential for balancing and harnessing prana to support overall well-being.

prati prasav: *Prati* means "again," and *prasav* means "birth" or "creation," so it translates to rebirth or spiritual re-creation. Often used to describe the spiritual practice of inner renewal, leading to higher states of consciousness or enlightenment.

raga: "Attachment" or "desire," which binds individuals to worldly pleasures and material pursuits.

Raktabija: A demon in Hindu scriptures whose blood, when spilled, gives rise to new demons, making him a formidable adversary. He symbolizes our never-ending thirst for materialistic pleasures.

Rama (Ram): A major deity in Hinduism, known as the seventh avatar of Vishnu. He symbolizes righteousness, courage, and devotion and is revered as a model of dharma.

Ramayana (Ramayan): An ancient Indian epic, detailing the life of Rama. It highlights themes of duty, virtue, and devotion.

Ravana: A demon king in Hindu mythology, notably the primary antagonist in the Ramayana. Ravana represents a complex character embodying both formidable strength and significant flaws.

Rudra granthi: A spiritual knot associated with Shiva that represents a blockage in energy flow and spiritual awakening, often located in the throat chakra.

sadhana: A disciplined spiritual practice aimed at personal growth and self-realization.

sakshatkar: Self-realization; the ultimate goal.

samadhi: A state of deep, meditative consciousness and spiritual absorption in yoga and Hinduism. This state is achieved through intense meditation and self-discipline, where the meditator experiences oneness with the object of meditation.

samarpan: Surrender to divine will.

samsara: The cycle of birth, death, and rebirth, driven by karma and attachments. The goal of spiritual seekers is to achieve liberation from this cycle.

samskara: "Impression" or "conditioning"; samskara highlights how past experiences shape and influence current life and spiritual progress.

sanatana parampara: The timeless and continuous spiritual practices and teachings passed down through generations. It highlights the preservation and continuity of spiritual wisdom and practices across ages.

sanchita karma: The accumulated actions and their consequences from past lives that affect one's current life, shaping present and future outcomes.

Sandhya kala: A period of time in the evening, considered auspicious in Hinduism, that usually begins around six and ends at ten at night.

Sanjeevani: "One that infuses life"; divine energy, representing healing and rejuvenation, celebrated for its legendary ability to restore life and vitality. It also refers to an herb known as *sanjivani buti* that brings the dead back to life.

sannyasa: The stage of renunciation in Hindu life, where one abandons worldly attachments to focus solely on spiritual pursuits.

satsang: A gathering or association with like-minded people or a guru (master) for spiritual discussion, reflection, initiation, and practice.

seva: "Service" (to mankind).

Shakti: The divine feminine energy in Hinduism, representing power and creativity. It is personified in various goddesses, such as Durga, Kali, Maa Laxmi, or Maa Sarswati, and drives the universe's dynamic forces.

shaktipat: "Descent of power" or "transfer of energy"; the transmission of spiritual energy from a guru to a disciple, aimed at awakening higher consciousness, to accelerate spiritual growth and realization. It often involves direct touch, gaze, or blessing from the guru.

Shambho: An epithet of Lord Shiva, meaning "Auspicious One" or "Benevolent One."

Shiva: A major Hindu deity known as the "destroyer" in the Trimurti, responsible for destruction and transformation. He is often depicted with a third eye and a snake around his neck.

Glossary

shivling: A sacred symbol of Lord Shiva, often represented as a cylindrical stone or pillar. It embodies Shiva's formless aspect and is a focus of worship in Hinduism.

Shiv Yog, Shiv Yogi: The term combines *shiva* (infinite) and *yog* (union or practice). Merging with the infinite is called Shiv Yog. A Shiv Yogi is one who follows the path of Shiv Yog, aiming for spiritual growth, self-realization, and union with divine consciousness.

shraddha: "Faith" or "trust"; denotes a deep, sincere commitment. It is essential for cultivating spiritual growth and sincerity in one's practice.

siddha: "Accomplished" or "perfected"; refers to a person who has attained a high level of spiritual realization, mastery, or accomplishment.

Sita: A central figure in the Ramayana, known as the wife of Lord Rama, who symbolizes virtue, devotion, and purity. She is revered for her strength and resilience in adversity.

sphatik shivling: A Shiva lingam made of crystal (*sphatik*) used in worship to enhance spiritual clarity and purity. It is known for its spiritual and healing properties.

sutra: "Thread" or "string"; symbolizing the connection of ideas. Sutra refers to a concise, aphoristic statement or text that encapsulates complex ideas or teachings.

Swami Vivekananda: A prominent Indian monk and a key figure in introducing Hindu philosophy to the Western world. Born in 1863, he was a disciple of Sri Ramakrishna.

Upanishads: Ancient Hindu texts that explore the nature of reality, the self (Atman), and ultimate truth (Brahman), forming a core part of Hindu philosophy.

Glossary

vaikhari: One of the four levels of speech; vaikhari is when you use your voice to tell what you're thinking.

Vedas: The most authoritative scriptures in Hinduism, encompassing various aspects of life and spirituality. There are four Vedas known as Rigveda, Samaveda, Yajurveda, and Atharvaveda. They include hymns, rituals, philosophy, and guidance on religious practices.

vidya: "Knowledge" or "wisdom"; vidya aims at acquiring insight and enlightenment, in both worldly and spiritual realms.

vish: Poison.

yagya (or yajna): A Vedic ritual of offerings accompanied by chanting of Vedic mantras. It is performed to invoke divine blessings, maintain cosmic order, and fulfill specific intentions.

yagyashala: A designated space or area where yagya (Vedic rituals and sacrifices) are performed.

yogi: One who is engaged in yoga practices for self-realization, spiritual growth, and physical well-being.

ACKNOWLEDGMENTS

Gratitude to my strength, my love, and my voice, my wife, Kavita Shivanand; my biggest support, whom I lovingly call boss, Ashok; and my divine brother, Jay.

Also, the team without which the book would not have been possible: Renée, Jaidree, and Ms. Sally for helping me find the right words.

And lastly, my most beautiful mother, who has silently always nudged me to the light.

ABOUT SHIV YOG AND YOGA OF IMMORTALS

SHIV YOG is an ancient lineage and spiritual tradition that traces its roots back to Adinath, the first guru, and continues through a long line of gurus up to Ishan Shivanand's father, Avdhoot Shivanand, and now Ishan himself as head guru.

Shiv Yog is focused on spiritual practices and meditation, rather than external ritual-based practices. At the core of Shiv Yog is the idea that one's own body and breath are the temple, rather than an external temple. God is the source of the infinite potential within every human being, and every human being has the potential to go beyond the limited identification with the body and mind.

Founded by Ishan Shivanand, **Yoga of Immortals** (YOI) brings the ancient spiritual practices and meditation techniques of the Shiv Yog lineage to the modern world, backing them with scientific evidence and making them accessible to everyone. It is an evidence-based mental wellness program clinically proven to enhance quality of life by reducing insomnia, stress, anxiety, and depression symptoms. Through deeper understanding of the cognitive aspects of yoga, YOI can help in improving energy as well as connecting more deeply and easily with oneself and others.

LEARN MORE:

Shiv Yog: https://shivyog.com/
Yoga of Immortals: https://yogaofimmortals.com/